24
HOURS
TO LIVE

24
HOURS
TO LIVE

Minton C. Johnston

ABINGDON PRESS / New York Nashville

24 HOURS TO LIVE

Copyright © 1963 by Abingdon Press

All rights in this book are reserved.
No part of the book may be reproduced in any
manner whatsoever without written permission of
the publishers except brief quotations embodied in
critical articles or reviews. For information address
Abingdon Press, Nashville 2, Tennessee.

Library of Congress Catalog Card Number: 63-14594

SET UP, PRINTED AND BOUND BY THE
PARTHENON PRESS AT NASHVILLE
TENNESSEE, UNITED STATES OF AMERICA

PREFACE

This book is a selection of messages made over a period of three years, broadcasting on Monday mornings a twelve-minute period called "Lift Up Your Hearts."

I am indebted to the Canadian Broadcasting Corporation for having given me the opportunity of delivering them and to Abingdon Press for believing they are worthy of a wider audience and for the privilege of having them published.

This, however, is in reality the third time they will have been presented. Every writer knows the necessity of having to read immediately to someone what he has written. I suffer from the same irrepressible urge. With the last tap of the typewriter I have to hurry down and in a spate of words (far different from the studied leisure of speaking before a microphone) spill it all to the most patient, the most encouraging, and fortunately at times the most stringent listener I have ever faced. You can guess who that is.

So to me they bear the stamp not only of radio messages but also of those first breathless readings, and because of that they seem to be almost as much hers as mine.

I can pay no other tribute to that listener than to dedicate this book to her—Ruth Eleanor Johnston, my wife.

MINTON C. JOHNSTON

CONTENTS

1

24 Hours to Live

I read about a man who discovered that he had less than twenty-four hours to live. It was particularly distressing because he was a young man in the pink of health and engaged in a very important work. Now he would be compelled to leave it to others to finish. The great problem here was that those who would be entrusted with the responsibility for carrying on his work seemed to be fearfully inadequate and lacking completely in understanding of what he had been trying to do.

Less than twenty-four hours to live! What would you or I have done had either of us been in his shoes?

With so much to do and so little time in which to do it I am sure the average person would do nothing but run around in small, hysterical, egocentric circles. He would probably just give up and moan and groan about how God is mistreating him and what a shame it is to die so young. If he gave any thought to his work at all he would probably just throw up his hands in despair. What would be the use of entrusting it to the others? They don't understand his goals and besides they are a selfish and ignorant lot, quite unfit to entrust with a delicate and dangerous task. It had been all he could do even while he was with them to keep them from quarreling—and he hadn't always succeeded at that—so how could he hope that they could carry on after he is dead? He might just as well write off his work as a failure.

It is a terrible thing to die knowing one is a failure, but what other course was there? With less than twenty-four hours left, if he hadn't succeeded in the previous thirty years, what could he possibly do now?

This wasn't an imaginary situation, a novel, or work of fiction. A real man faced exactly that problem. His name was Jesus.

That has spoiled it! You may turn away disappointedly and say, "Oh, Jesus! That's different." The whole point, however, of the gospel is that it wasn't different. Jesus was a young man; he did have a most important work to do which apparently had been a failure up to a certain point; and there was a time when he had just learned that he had less than twenty-four hours to live.

Of the crowds which had followed him only a handful remained, and they were so pig-headed and so self-centered that they could not—or would not—grasp the basic principles he had been trying to establish. Ambitious for power, they were always quarreling among themselves as to who was the most important. Competent judges declared that they were "unlearned and ignorant men." Besides they were cowards, as the morrow would soon prove.

Yet if the important work Jesus had undertaken was to be finished it would have to be completed by them, for there was no one else to do it, and Jesus had less than a day to live. It was now evening. By noon the next day he would be dying, by three o'clock he would be dead.

The Gospel is trying to tell us that while we may call Jesus Son of God and realize his divinity, we must also hold fast to this tremendous fact that while on earth he was a *man*—a man engaged in a vital work, a young man who once had only twenty-four hours to live, and a man who lived these hours victoriously. Chapters 13 through 17 of the Gospel of John not only tell the story, they give the very atmosphere of the Upper Room. You can almost see what is happening.

First of all Jesus did that difficult, and to us almost impossible, thing; he forgot himself, his apparent failure, and the tragedy which loomed so near at hand. In the four or five hours of that evening he set about doing what he had been unable to do in the previous thirty years—and he did it.

As I read, I was reminded of the professor of surgery who told his class, "Gentlemen, be very careful in this operation. If you sever this artery the patient will bleed to death in three minutes. But don't worry, gentlemen. You can sew it up again in a minute and a half, if you don't hurry."

"If you don't hurry," that is exactly the impression I get of Jesus in the Upper Room, of his calm, unhasting serenity, of his workmanlike use of the time available. The disciples had burst into the room, jostling one another for the chief places, bitter with jealousy and suspicion. The presence of Judas the betrayer cast a gloom over them all as if the poison of his hatred had somehow infected them. The cloud of the coming tragedy settled unconsciously on every mind. Jesus had only four hours in which to combat all that and lay the foundation which would make the carrying on of his work possible. He had only those hours, but they were enough.

There is one thing we ought to get into our minds too—that our time is also enough, if we don't hurry. The real question, though, is: Time enough for what? When we have only twenty-four hours left it will be too late to decide what things are

11

important, what things we simply must finish, and what can be left undone. That is the reason for bringing the whole matter up now. We simply must get it straight before there is any crisis to confuse our thinking and panic our hearts. When the time does come all this will have been decided already or it will be too late to decide anything.

Personally when the time does come I would like to have some work that was unfinished and which was important enough to finish. It would be awful to have everything cleaned up long before and be just sitting around waiting for the end. Surely that would mean that I had not found anything particularly important to do, not only then but at any time during my life. What a tragedy it would be never to have anything really worth doing!

Twenty-four hours to live sounds ominous. That depends, however, on where we put the emphasis. If we stress the last word and understand what the word "live" means, then it can be like an army moving to battle, like crusaders lifting their cross-emblazoned banners, or like Jesus in the Upper Room. That is what the chapters in John cry out to us and what, from the space he gave them, they said to John too. In the Upper Room Jesus came alive for John as he never had before. Jesus had twenty-four hours to live and how he lived them!

We also want to live. We crave for something beyond mere existence. Breathing, eating, and sleeping aren't enough; we want to *live*. Our trouble is that we have too many days and months and years. We don't feel the urgency to live each twenty-four hours as though they were our last. Yet, after all, that *is* all we have, not that we are going to die tomorrow, though we might quite easily. All we ever have is today, trite though that statement is. If we can't live today we probably won't live any day, and most certainly we won't really live on that last day, that day when there will be only twenty-four hours left.

What would make us really live today or any day? To me there are three things which make a life as opposed to an existence: a leader worth following, a task worth doing, and a meaning and purpose to life itself. Those would be worth living for, because, strange as it may seem, they are worth dying for.

Those were the things which counted with Jesus—that he had a Father in heaven whom he loved, that he had found on earth something worth dying for and therefore something on which he could and did spend his life as well as his death, and that for him life had a supreme meaning and purpose so that not even the cross was defeat nor the years of the ministry which led up to it wasted.

That was his secret of life, which made the twenty-four hours such a triumph, and which presented a picture of life lived as it had never been lived before. Surely then it is the secret by which you and I can make every twenty-four hours, not just the last ones, really worth living too.

2
Movings and Fires

My mother used to quote a saying of her grandmother's, "Three movings are as bad as a fire." I used to think the saying meant three movings destroyed as much as a fire. I imagined movers banging up the dining-room table, dropping the best dinner plates, and losing forever some small but valuable trinkets. Three movings to my mind just about finished everything one had. Then a few years ago mother told me what it meant to her mind, that three movings got rid of as much accumulated junk as a fire.

What a mass of things we do accumulate in attic, cellar, and all through the house! We never realize how much there is until we have to move or a fire gets rid of it for us. But there is one good thing about moving as compared to a fire. When we move *we* have to do the sorting ourselves. *We* have to decide what to keep and what to throw away, what is important enough to save and what we can cheerfully give to the trash man.

It is a good thing once in a while to have to move just so that one is compelled to consider the value of each possession. And the farther off one moves or the smaller the next house, then the more real and important the problem becomes. You can't take everything, so what will you take? How do you select which is valuable and which isn't? It is usually fairly easy to discover what is trash. The very necessity to move reveals that. You come across something and exclaim, "Goodness! Why did I ever keep that?" and out it goes. Of course if you weren't going to move you would still keep it, cluttering up your home and your life with it.

It is far more difficult, however, to choose between things which each have value. It is not a question now of one being trash; these are both things we can use, things which help make life easier and more pleasant. But we can't take them both. Which will we take, which discard? What standard are we to use to determine the answer?

This kind of decision faces us all constantly. Not that we are all going to move. It would be easier if we were. Nor does it primarily concern possessions and things, for that decision is an easier one to make. The choice which faces us all constantly is between various values in life itself.

For instance there was the young lady who came into my office. During our conversation she said she had always wanted to be a doctor. It was her one ambition in life, but here she was a clerk in a jewelry store. Why hadn't she become a doctor? Because she had been unable to choose between various good and valuable things in life. She liked good clothes, a regular salary, going out with her boy friends, and all the pleasurable activities of a young lady. They were all innocent and valuable, every single one of them, but she couldn't have them and a medical course too. So without meaning to she had made her decision. Of course she didn't realize or accept that. She blamed the world, circumstances, fate. But they weren't to blame. It was just her inability to choose between values. So because she did not have enough strength of mind to make the decision, it was decided for her, and that which she inwardly thought to be the most valuable of all was lost.

The same idea occurs in a rather preposterous story in the Old Testament. It was intended to be preposterous. A prophet made it up. He pretended to be a soldier who had been given charge of an important captive and had lost him. He went to King Ahab and said, "As thy servant was busy here and there, he was gone." The king flew into a rage and would have killed the supposed soldier, but the prophet revealed his identity and proclaimed the curse of God on Ahab for letting escape from punishment a man delivered by God into his hand. It is hardly conceivable that a soldier could be really so remiss, but that preposterous statement is often true in life. "While thy servant was busy here and there, he was gone." While we are occupied with many important and worthwhile endeavors something even more important escapes us:

> For of all sad words of tongue or pen,
> The saddest are these: "It might have been!"

Something escaped, a value disappeared, a treasured ideal vanished, a cherished ambition faded, so often simply because we were busy here and there, occupied with other things. We did not deliberately sit down and choose to let it go. It happened without our really realizing it. Once in a while when we move we have to face the problem of choosing between our possessions and treasures, but constantly we must choose between values in life. Again I ask, what is the standard to be?

Livingstone had one, "I will place no value," he said, "on anything I have or may possess except in relation to the Kingdom of Christ." Well, we might say, that was all right for Livingstone. He was traveling through Africa, always on the move, always having to limit his baggage. But what we forget is that he chose to be on the move. He deliberately decided to open up Africa to the gospel. Is Livingstone's standard too high for you? Thank God it was not too high for Jesus. He placed no value on throne or power or position or even on life itself except in relation to you and me. If that standard is too high what other will you choose? May I suggest one? The standard of the *longest value* and the *greatest usefulness*. How lasting is the value; how great, compared to everything else, is its usefulness?

Jesus told a story about a man who made a decision. He was very rich, with fields heavy with crops. He decided to pull down his barns and build greater ones and then when they were filled to live happily ever after. Unfortunately that night he died. Barns and crops were then of no value to him. He entered the other world without possessions and with nothing useful at all. So also it was with the Rich Young Ruler who went away sad because he had great possessions. He had to decide between eternal life with poverty or this life with wealth. Jesus forced the decision on him. In that the young man was fortunate, at least *he* had to make the decision.

Have you decided? Granted all the things you do and have are valuable and important, how long will they last and how really useful are they to you? There is one last move you and I will have to make, we'll have to move from this life to the next. Then there is only one thing we can take—ourselves. Whether our life will be trash or infinitely valuable we will have decided long before. For only as we take the gift of eternal life in Jesus Christ—take it deliberately—will there be any value to us at all. That decision you and I have to make now.

17

3

Servants

In our house at Thornhill, just north of Toronto, we live
beside a cemetery which goes back to the early eighteen hundreds when this part of Ontario was first settled. I walk through it
ever so often, especially on Sunday mornings before church, and
look at the tombstones. There are some in particular which I
stop and look at again and again. They have historical interest,
though it is purely local, and carry the mind back to pioneer days
and early struggles.

There is a stone for Colonel Moodie, whose courage I ad-
mire even though I am dubious about his common sense. He
attempted to ride through a gathering of rebels to warn "Muddy
York" (as Toronto was then named) in the local rebellion of
1837. He didn't make it. So for 126 years he has rested quietly
next door. Then there is the cairn raised to John Willson, who
had the first lease on "The Old Mill," a familiar Toronto land-
mark, long ruined, and was held prisoner in Fort York in 1813
when the Americans burned York, later called Toronto, in
revenge for the burning of Washington. There is a very imposing
monument to the Rev. George Mortimer, the first rector of the
Anglican church, who died in 1844 when his horse ran away
with him. Other stones tell of pioneers gone these hundred and
more years, the inscriptions almost indecipherable with age.

My favorite memorial, though, is one which could easily be over-
looked. It is on the back of the monument to the Rev. George

Mortimer and his family. It is very brief but to my mind singularly touching. It reads simply, "Also in memory of Frances Doughty, whose faithful service of forty-five years was only terminated by the death of her mistress. 'Well done good and faithful servant.' "

Whenever I walk around looking at the tombstones I always come back to that one and stand silently before it. It seems to me the noblest and finest of them all.

I don't know any more about Frances Doughty. I wish I did. Was she a maid or a cook? Where did she come from and what happened to her afterwards? I don't know. She must have been a very young girl when she first came into the minister's household in England, fifteen years or so before they emigrated to Canada. She saw the children born and some of them die. She watched her mistress change from a bride to a matron and from a matron to an old woman. Forty-five years a servant, forty-five years of dusting and washing dishes, of looking after children and answering doorbells, of getting up before dawn to light the great wood stoves, and of going around at night to see that all the doors and windows were safely bolted.

Imagine those forty-five years of servitude, of low pay (for what servant's pay was not low in those days?), of the one afternoon a week and every other Sunday to herself, or of whatever arrangement for the pitifully meager free time a servant then received. Were "followers" discouraged, and was that why she always remained plain Frances Doughty? I wonder how she stood those forty-five years of being a servant. This I know, she couldn't have stood it unless there had been a stronger bond than the usual one between mistress and servant. There must have been a deep and abiding affection. Indeed the memorial

19

suggests that. Even in death they are permanently linked, for the bond which held them was love.

Today we don't like the word servant. It smacks to us of slavery. We shudder at servitude, at being under someone and compelled to obey his orders. We demand the right to be our own masters, to have freedom and equality and independence. We refuse to be called servants.

What a lot we have missed! That revulsion has tended to spoil our religion. I don't mean just that it has handicapped and hampered the work of Christ and his church, though it has done that too. I mean that it has handicapped and hampered us, that it has robbed us of the full joy of Christianity. I know of nothing which has done it more. We like to look on ourselves as equal partners with God, as his freeborn children, and his spiritual advisers. We do what we want to do, give what we care to give, and then expect his cordial and humble gratitude for whatever we have condescended to do for him. We resent Paul's words, "know ye not that . . . ye are not your own? For ye are bought with a price." Even more we resent Jesus' term "servants" when we realize that it meant bond slaves. Like the Jews we cry out that we are free!

Poor Frances Doughty, we think. What did she get out of life? Forty-five years a servant! Forty-five years of obeying orders—what a tragedy that seems to us. But the memorial shouts to us that it was not a tragedy but a triumph. There it is on the back of that tombstone, brief and dignified, breathing something so many of us have missed—love. That's what she got out of it, something no money can buy and no independence can equal.

Can there ever be any true love without accepting to some degree the role of servant? I am sure that there can't. Whenever in marriage or in a family or anywhere else there is an insistence on equality, on getting all one's rights, on receiving an equal share, then love never reaches its full heights, and all too often it withers and dies. I remember as a boy the heartburning whenever there was something to be divided among the three of us, say a piece of cake. Each was sure that he got the smallest piece. Even when one of us divided it it was agony—trying to be fair, and yet not to get the worst of it. The flavor of the cake was always a little bitter from envy and jealousy.

Well, isn't the flavor of the cake in the world today bitter with envy and jealousy too, whether it is the cake capital and labor seek to divide, the one the nations seek to share, or, most of all, the cake we wish to divide with God? It is in the last we suffer most. Where the triumphs could be so great and the rewards so sweet, there is only dissatisfaction and bitterness; just because we demand independence, clamor for equality, and refuse to be thought of as servants.

Yet despite our clamor we are servants, for we *have* been bought with a price and we belong not to ourselves but to God. This is a fact which we must face and accept, or all of life will be made acid with rebellion and bitter with disappointment. After all God himself accepted that fact. He "took upon him the form of a servant," wrote Paul of Jesus in Phil. 2:7, and the highest name for the coming Messiah in Isaiah was "the suffering servant." What Jesus did for us was to redeem us. That means to buy us back. He didn't make us free and independent. He bought us for God. We became the slaves and servants of God instead of what we had been. Our choice is not then between being servants or being free. It is simply a question of servitude —being servants of God or of other things.

21

The strangest thing about this servant business is that we find our true liberty when we accept the fact, however reluctantly, that we are and never can escape from being servants. That was true of Jesus. In Phil. 2 Paul describes Jesus' acceptance of all that being a servant meant—giving up the throne, taking human form, becoming obedient unto death, even the death of the cross —then he cries, "Wherefore God also hath highly exalted him, and given him a name which is above every name." Why? Because he was born to the divine purple and had a right to inherit the throne? No. Because he was the most perfect servant the world has seen.

Do you want to find the real joy of religion? Then accept the fact that you are not your own, that you have been bought, and that you are therefore a servant of God. Then Jesus can say to you as he did to the disciples, "Henceforth I call you not servants; . . . but . . . friends." The servant is transformed when his service becomes the service of love. Then, like Frances Doughty, he will take his place in the pride and love and the family of the Master forever.

4

Self-denial

In some churches it is the custom to deny yourself something you especially like for the forty days of Lent, something like candy, beefsteaks, or ice cream. But to do this is of value only if it is something you are very fond of, which to give up is a trial. Then it is a very useful practice.

Giving up something you like is called self-denial, and one religious group has what they call a "self-denial week." While I agree that it is a good idea to deny yourself something, I am just wondering whether this is really equivalent to self-denial. I am thinking of that rather stern verse where Jesus warned the disciples in these words, "If any man will come after me, let him deny himself, and take up his cross daily, and follow me." Does "deny himself" mean the same thing as denying yourself something? I don't think so. The New English Bible doesn't think so either, for it translates it this way, "If anyone wishes to be a follower of mine, *he must leave self behind.*"

You know, in the light of the warning of Jesus, with its emphasis on the cross which loomed up ahead of him and threatened all who dared to follow him, giving up candy for forty days seems a bit trivial, doesn't it? In fact when death—a shameful, torturing death—is an immediate prospect, most things seem trivial. You then get down to the fundamentals of life, and you weigh everything carefully—ambitions, hopes, family, friends, the blue sky and the sunshine, the sound of rain on the roof and all the little everyday things which have become so dear. It is the choice of a condemned man waiting for the dawn when he must die who knows that by one word of recanting he can have life again, can feel the arms of his loved ones about him, can look forward to the days stretching ahead. Life or death, that's it, life or death.

The disciples had to face this literally, just as Jesus himself faced it. Jesus knew that to continue on the course he had set for himself meant inevitable death. Peter might not be able to understand and all the others might think he was a fool, but Jesus knew. To be the Messiah was to die. It would be to die in our world today too. And if they killed Jesus, then the same fate awaited those who followed him. That was a fact they simply had to face. It wasn't any theoretical question, it was a stern reality. To follow Jesus meant to court death, and of the twelve who listened to him it was true of all but John. They paid with their lives for following him.

It was in that context that Jesus said what he did about taking up a cross. Sometimes we hear people talk about their crosses when they mean a hasty temper or a nagging family or a physical handicap. "It is my cross," they say, but it isn't a cross. In modern terms they wouldn't dream of saying, "It's my electric chair," or "It's my scaffold."

For most of us today, in the Western World at least, that verse just doesn't apply. We aren't going to be hanged, electrocuted, gassed, or crucified for being Christians. We aren't even going to be shot. We are going to go on living quite ordinary lives without any particular risk or danger. True in some cases friends may laugh at us and in other extreme cases families may disown us, but they are most unusual. For the majority of us it will simply mean a happier, fuller life, and we will be quite displeased if it doesn't mean greater health, longer life, enriched personalities, and personal riches. It is certainly a far cry from the time of the disciples to our position today.

Well then, if that verse about the cross no longer applies literally to us, what about those words about denying ourselves? Do they apply today, or are they just part of a cruel past, fortunately no longer confronting us?

Deny *yourself*, not deny yourself something. But what does "leave self behind" mean? Just this, you can't be selfish and be a Christian. Selfish, that's a word which needs thinking about, dissecting, emphasizing. To deny yourself means to stop being *selfish*. I believe that both parts of the twenty-fourth verse of Matt. 16 still apply today as truly as then. If we are to be followers of Christ who went open-eyed to the cross, we also must be willing and ready to die for him, and we must also "deny ourselves," "leave self behind," stop being selfish.

When I first became a minister I took several church services at a psychiatric hospital, though I think then we called it the asylum. During the succeeding thirty-five years or so I've been thinking, puzzling, and wondering about mental illness. What causes it? Why do some get it and others not? Each time I went to the hospital I'd ask the doctors. They muttered learnedly but finally had to confess they didn't know. Then a couple of years ago I had a chance to talk to a distinguished psychiatrist whom I used to know when he was a boy. This time I put the question in a different way and just blurted out, "Tell me, Leslie, how much does selfishness have to do with mental illness?" Quick as a flash his answer came back, "Almost everything."

That's what I suspected. That's where the devils get in. The

Bible described mental illness as people becoming possessed by the devil. Does that sound too old-fashioned? Then just think for a moment of another side of the matter, of all the rottenness which is in the world, of all the devilishness there is around, and of all the evils, if you prefer it that way. Where do they come from? What gives them their power? What lets them in to wreak such havoc? In every case you know of, isn't it just plain selfishness? In sober truth I know of no misery, no evil, and no shame which hasn't selfishness as its root cause.

The psychiatrists, however, would probably turn to me and shake their fingers and say, "Don't you know, you preacher, that one of the three main causes of mental disorder is religion?" I'll take their word for it, for I can well believe it, but it doesn't alter the situation in the slightest degree. Religion can be as selfish as anything else. Hasn't most of our emphasis unfortunately been upon what people can get out of religion? Haven't we been hammering at them to save their souls? Haven't we held out promises of reward—from health, wealth, and happiness to an assured heaven of perfect pleasure and eternal bliss?

Of course those things *are* promised and we have every right to urge people to find them. Our great sin has been that we haven't pointed out clearly and unmistakably that they are entirely dependent on finding something else without which they are valueless. We are like parents urging a girl to marry a millionaire and so find security, a beautiful home, and all the things the heart can crave. But the heart doesn't crave those things at all, it craves love. Without love life can and so often does become a horror and a nightmare no matter how great our possessions may be.

The reward of finding God is above all love, his love for

us and our love for him. The promise of Jesus is even more true in the realm of the spirit than it is in material things, "Seek ye first the kingdom of God, and his righteousness; and all these things shall be added unto you." That brings us back to where we came in. To find Jesus you have to "deny yourself," "leave self behind." That is the only gateway to love on earth or in heaven.

5

Incurable?

Most signs I just don't see or pay much attention to, but there are others which give me the jitters. There are lights which are too bright, arrows which flash red just past a traffic light, and jiggly, nervous signs. I notice those. What is worse I keep on noticing them. I'll be driving quite happily along when something inside says, "It's coming!" and I am ill at ease until that sign looms into view, makes me uncomfortable again with its dancing, and then is swept behind, ready to pounce on me again the next time I drive by. There is one on the way up to the lake, a completely inoffensive sign on a barn. But it is cute, too terribly cute, and I shudder every time I pass. Last time it was a dark night and I sighed with relief. I wouldn't have to see that sign. But even the darkness didn't work. I knew exactly when I came to it, unseen though it was, and I shuddered again.

There used to be a sign on Bloor Street in Toronto that made me more than shudder. It made me angry. It made me boil. Yet it was intended as a kindly sign. Somebody had started the place and made the sign in the spirit of charity and love and helpfulness. I'm sure that the place did a marvelous work. But for me the sign ruined it all. That sign read, "Home for Incurable Children." What a wonderful gesture and what a horrible thought. Imagine what the boys and girls who went into it and who lived there felt, always being stigmatized by that tragic word—incurable. It was even worse, surely, for the people who had to put them there, their fathers and mothers, their brothers and sisters. What a terrible realization to come to anyone that "our Johnny is incurable, you know, so we had to put him in the *Home for Incurable Children*." I've been near enough to that myself to feel the horror of it as no one else can who hasn't been there. But worst of all, what about the doctors, the nurses, and society itself? Must we imply some people are incurable, so all we can do is put them away, out of sight, out of mind? We'll make it as easy and pleasant as we can for them, of course, but after all they are incurable; so let's forget them and get on with other things.

Whenever I used to pass that fine building into which I've never entered I felt like screaming out to someone, to anyone, "How dare you! Who do you think you are, God? How dare you say they are incurable?"

It was the superintendent of nurses at the Brantford Hospital who made me realize that first, God bless her. I came by her office after visiting a patient for what I believed was the last time. She saw me, called for me to come in, and asked whom I'd been seeing. I told her and mournfully added that the patient had only six hours to live. She burst out at me with a sternness of which I would never thought her capable. "Never say that!" she cried. "Never." I protested that the doctors had said so. "They don't know," she cried out again, "they can't know. Only God knows."

Rebuked and chastened, I went away, but not to forget. That was something I could never forget, for the superintendent was right. The patient didn't die that day or that week or that month. The doctors didn't know.

An experience in my own family brought this home to me.

29

Three weeks before my father died he called my brother and me into the room where he was confined with what seemed to be just a mild attack of grippe. "You'll have to represent me at Cyrus' funeral," he said to us. "He can't live more than a day." Fortunately he didn't say what day. It was a day, forty-two years later, that my father's twin brother died. The old gentleman was ninety-six. During the intervening years I personally know of at least six occasions, and heard of as many more, when the doctors said my uncle couldn't possibly live through the night. Well, they were right, he did die—at ninety-six. In that sense we are all incurable.

But we aren't incurable in the way the sign meant, in the way the doctors spoke of my uncle, in the way a great many people think about themselves. We aren't incurable in that way.

I suppose in a sense I'm twisting things a little. I don't mean that there aren't some conditions for which at the moment the cure hasn't been found, though it will be in time. There are lame people, blind people, sick people, who may always have the symptoms and the handicaps of their conditions. But I still say, in spite of what they have, in spite of the handicap, that they aren't incurable. There is more to them surely than legs which won't work, eyes which don't see, or bodies which are sick. Perhaps the very handicap will make something else work better, and the handicap itself will in a sense be a cure.

I think, for instance, of John Milton dreaming for years of writing a poem which would, as he wrote,

> . . . assert Eternal Providence,
> and justify the ways of God to men.

Then he went completely and incurably blind. His sonnet "On His Blindness" is the cry of a shaken soul:

> When I consider how my light is spent
>> Ere half my days in this dark world and wide,
>> And that one talent which is death to hide
>> Lodged with me useless, though my soul more bent
> To serve therewith my Maker, and present
>> My true account, lest He returning chide.

What a tragedy for a poet! How impossible to do anything, we might say. But blind as he was he wrote or rather dictated "Paradise Lost," the greatest poem of its kind in the world. Incurable? Maybe. But though physically there was no cure, perhaps the eyes of the body were shut that the eyes of the soul might see.

Something like that crossed my mind as I walked along Bloor Street the other day. I had noticed a few years earlier that the large sign I hated had been relegated to a corner. But the other day, shuddering as I neared it, I lifted my eyes to see that it was gone entirely. It was wiped out, forgotten. In its place another was raising its triumphant banner and proclaiming its faith. "The House of Happiness," it read. What a tremendous achievement of the spirit that was, to change "The Home for Incurable Children" into "The House of Happiness."

I'm going to remember that sign now. I'll glow all over whenever I think of it. But surely it is not enough, to bask in someone else's faith. It is not enough unless it inspires me to the same kind of faith. After all isn't that what Jesus came into the world to do, to change what men call incurable? Isn't that what he did with the cross? Isn't that what he is trying to do with you and me? It is when he does it that men really see the power and glory of God. Make no mistake about it, it isn't easy. No, but it can be done. That change of "The Home for Incurable Children" into "The House of Happiness" proves it. Surely if it was done there it can be done with you and me also.

6

When You're Lost

In her book about the Maine woods, *We Took to the Woods,* Louise Dickenson Rich tells of striking off one day for B Pond and getting lost on the way back. It was a familiar path which she had often taken, but this time the whole way was confused with windrows of brush and fallen trees left from the 1938 hurricane. She struggled along, climbing over, under, and around the tree trunks, till suddenly she discovered she had not the faintest idea where she was, where B Pond was, or where Forest Lodge was. She was completely lost.

As I read it I felt some of the panic which comes to a lost person, that unreasoning terror which makes him take to his heels and run frantically, anywhere. I don't suppose there is any more terrible fear in the world than that. Imagine it for yourself. Just sit down and think of yourself as being lost. All around are the limitless reaches of the forest. Somewhere is the place you started from, somewhere the place you want to reach. But where?

Perhaps you can remember being lost. I can, twice. Once was in the city. It probably was one of the very first times I went down town alone. I came out of a department store and had not the faintest idea where I was. I was on a street, but what street? Which was north? Which south? Where was my home? My heart came into my mouth and for a moment panic seized me. Then common sense prevailed. I simply went back into the store and got my directions straight again. After all I did know where the books were, the jewelry, and the boys' trousers.

The second time was in England. Returning to London from an air station near Bristol in a blackout several of us got on the wrong road somehow, a Roman road by the way (maybe its straightness confused us). There we were, on top of the world it seemed, with no idea where the road went. There was a man leaning on a gate and we persuaded the driver to stop and ask directions. The man came to the car. Unfortunately he had a cleft palate, but the undistinguishable words did something for us. We choked down our fears and went along the road, and it brought us out all right.

To get back to Mrs. Rich lost in the Maine woods, she had been persuaded by her man of all work to take a compass with her on her hike. "Remember," he advised, "it's right. A compass is always right, remember that." She had thought that a rather silly piece of advice at the time and so, when in her panic she remembered the compass and took it out, she was sure it was pointing in exactly the wrong direction. She was going to throw it away when the words came back to her, "A compass is always right, remember that." But it couldn't be! Other compasses maybe, for other people perhaps, but this one was so wrong that any fool would know it.

Again her hand was lifted to toss the useless compass away when a fraction of sanity returned. Maybe it was she who was the fool. Perhaps, even if it *was* all wrong, she ought to give it a chance. Reluctantly she decided to follow it. It was like pulling teeth, for every instinct rebelled against going in the direction it pointed. But she made herself do it and after two hours of desperation she came suddenly to the edge of the forest to see

Forest Lodge just across the river. The compass had been right after all.

Getting lost is not just something that happens to us in woods or on roads and streets. Jesus implied that in Luke 15 when he talked about a lost sheep and a lost boy. They were lost in different ways, but the boy was just as lost as the sheep, though he was lost in the sense which Paul used in I Cor. 4 when he said that the gospel was hid "to them that are lost." When used in that sense the word "lost" may seem confusing but the idea is really quite simple. You are lost spiritually when you don't know where you are, where you have been, or where you are going. I've met many people who were lost, even though they didn't know it. I've been like that myself. So I'd like from my own experience to give a little advice to others, advice I also want to hang onto for myself.

First, realize that you *are* lost. This is no admission of defeat, it is just common sense. If most people realized it soon enough, they could easily find their way out. Don't let foolish pride, fear of criticism, or the scorn of people more lost than yourself fool you. The moment you feel lost or even the least confused stand still. Say to yourself, "Maybe I'm lost. Now what shall I do?" (God has two great difficulties with people; first, to get them to acknowledge that they *are* lost, and second to get them to realize that *he* can find the way out for them. If they'd only realize the first in time, *he* could do the second so much easier.)

The second bit of advice is this: Go back, if you can, to some familiar place. That's what I did at the store and I think I was wise. Do the same in your mind. Go back to the time you went to church with your parents, to your mother saying the bedtime prayer, to the kindergarten when you sang, "Jesus Loves Me."

There you are in familiar and safe surroundings. Retrace your steps. Where did you leave the path? Where did you turn aside just a yard or two because it was easier going or because some flowers of pleasure beckoned you just a little off the way? Well, that's the place. Now take the right road, openly acknowledging that you went astray. Call it repentance if you like, but it is after all plain common sense. In the woods or in life, it is simply getting on the right path again.

The third thing I want to say is that if you are on the road and you find you have made no real digression from it then keep on going. I know the night is dark, the surroundings are strange and terrifying, and the road ahead is unfamiliar. Many people, however, think they are lost when they are only frightened. If you are on the road keep on going. All roads, after all, do end somewhere.

There are a tremendous number of us who have to walk unfamiliar and difficult roads—roads which terrify, roads full of sorrow and suffering. But once we are on the road we have to keep going. We walk by faith and not by sight, as Paul said, and the faith is simply this: Trust in the One who made the road. It does lead somewhere. Don't be fooled by the people around us. There are a great many others who are beset by doubts and near to panic through fear. We aren't the only ones, so keep on going. We surely can trust God who made the road. After all it was his feet which beat it out.

The fourth bit of advice is similar. Trust your compass. "Chart and compass come from Thee," wrote Edward Hopper in the hymn "Jesus, Saviour, Pilot Me." That is the way he pilots, his compass is the Bible. Usually we take that Book for granted. But when we are lost we look at it and it may seem that our compass is wrong. But it isn't. Remember what the man said, "A compass is always right, remember that." Our compass is always right too. It doesn't matter what we think, how we feel, what our emotions are, or what our reason and intelligence say. When one is lost, all these are liars of the first order. The compass is *always* right.

If we'll follow that we can forget all the other advice. We do have a compass which has guided millions of lost souls home. The Bible has led them through darkness and terror, through sorrow and suffering, through persecution and martyrdom. It worked with them, then did it suddenly go wrong when it came into our hands? No! If it has led so many others to safety it can also lead us. But we have to trust it and follow it. If we do we need never be lost.

7
Following Directions

Louise Dickenson Rich wrote about knitting in *We Took to the Woods*. She was a good knitter, she said, one who did fancy stitches, intricate patterns, and complicated designs; the kind of knitting, I imagine, which leaves people like me completely bewildered as to how anyone can do it. Mrs. Rich said she did it mostly by following printed directions. That too seemed to baffle most of her friends. They declared *they* could not possibly follow a pattern. Show them how and they could do it, or they might even work it out themselves from the completed garment, but printed directions, no.

Mrs. Rich sniffed at that. To her mind that attitude was plain silly. She declared there was nothing difficult about following printed directions. The trouble with people who said they couldn't do it was that they tried to understand them. They tried to relate the first steps to the finished article, and when there was no obvious relationship, they got discouraged and quit. Then Mrs. Rich made a challenging statement. "You don't have to understand directions," she wrote. "All you have to do is follow them. . . . What you need is not intelligence but blind faith." She herself, she said, never read the directions beyond the operation she was engaged in, having a simple trust that the person who wrote the directions knew what he was doing.

I was impressed with that. When first I read it I had just finished building a boat. Now I'm not a boat builder or really very much of a carpenter, except in a very rough and ready way. Anything like cabinet making leaves me gasping with awe. But I built that boat. I had to. I wanted a boat and the only way for a preacher to get one is to build it himself. I didn't build it from kits either, for that also was way out of reach financially, but from raw lumber and nails and screws and with a set of plans and instructions.

I admit I had misgivings, but not nearly as many as my family had. To them and me it seemed ridiculous to think of *me* building a boat. But I started out, one step at a time, not looking beyond the operation I was engaged in (nor daring to), hoping desperately that the man who drew the plans knew what he was doing and knew also what a clumsy amateur I was. There were times when I could easily have thrown the whole thing over, when the plans seemed senseless, when I made foolish mistakes, when the mess in the garage looked less like a boat than a jumble of wood. But I worked and worried through those times and the boat was built.

Like Mrs. Rich's knitting it turned out all right. Not to be too modest, it turned out wonderfully. All the real credit, however, goes to the man who drew the plans, and only a little to me for having sense enough to follow them, even when I didn't understand them—which was most of the time.

So you see how Mrs. Rich's words rang a bell with me. "You don't have to understand directions, all you need to do is follow them." Right. "What you need is not intelligence but blind faith." Right again. Intelligence and skill I didn't have, but if I was going to have a boat at all blind faith was what I certainly needed. "Simple trust that the person who wrote [the directions] knew what he was doing." I knew the name at the bottom of those plans. I felt I could trust him. And I was right, I could. My main concern here, however, is not knitting nor boats but life. How does what Mrs. Rich wrote apply here? I agree with Mrs. Rich that trust is a very important thing to discover, perhaps the most important of all. She said if she taught her children nothing else she was going to teach them that.

Do you know how to follow directions? It is surprising how many people don't. When it comes to life and religion so many tend to throw over all they know and practice in knitting or boat building. They play down blind faith and simple trust and put their emphasis on intelligence and understanding. When they don't understand, or their intelligence has led them into difficulties, they get discouraged. But surely it is in building a life and finding God that we need to follow the directions most of all.

Perhaps it boils down to the question of directions. In a book of instructions about knitting we know someone wrote it who presumably knew what she was doing. On a set of boat plans we see a naval architect's name and presume he knew what he was doing too. What about life? What about religion? Are they just chance and guesswork? Did someone make plans there too, or is it all just a crazy jumble, as Macbeth declared at the end of all his scheming and manipulating,

> Life's . . . a tale
> Told by an idiot, full of sound and fury,
> Signifying nothing.

You have to take your choice. You can presume that life is more than chance, more than a merry-go-round getting nowhere. You can choose to pin your faith on the Bible, believing with it that even a cross is not a meaningless and tragic form but an instrument fitting into the divine purpose and revealing the divine will. Or else you can presume there is no meaning to life and no pattern, no beginning and no end. If the latter is the case neither faith nor trust, my words nor your own intelligence, can help you. You are sunk. Personally I must follow an inner instinct, a compelling conviction that there is a pattern to life and a set of directions written by One I can trust.

After all you don't have to go far in life to discover what a small role intelligence plays in the great decisions and that accident can't describe them at all. We often view with awe the outcome of following where Someone who had made a pattern led us. Take Mrs. Rich herself. She lived in the Maine woods because she had once gone there on a vacation canoe trip.

The end of that trip led her up the Carry Road and she came to a newly opened camp just as a man came out of the door of a cabin to split a bit of kindling to light his first fire.

Literally one moment earlier she would have missed him, one moment later and he would have gone in again. The precise moment of her arrival, out of all time, changed the whole course of her life, for he was the man she was to marry.

Haven't we all gone through the same kind of thing? I have. I am amazed as I look back at how I have been led. It has not been a matter of my intelligence at all. I couldn't understand, for it was completely dark to me. But in the very darkness God was most at work and in the seeming accidents of life I later discovered his hand.

The Jews had a word, "Ebenezer," about which we used to sing, shouting loudly:

> Here I raise mine Ebenezer;
>   Hither by Thy help I'm come;
> And I hope, by Thy good pleasure,
>   Safely to arrive at home.
>   —ROBERT ROBINSON

Ebenezer was a cairn which Samuel raised saying, "Hitherto hath the Lord helped us." Yes, hitherto, up to this mark, unto this day, hitherto. Did God stop suddenly then? Are the assurances of the past for the past only? Or if we can see a pattern up to now, doesn't that pattern carry on into the darkness of tomorrow?

Yes, I think Mrs. Rich's advice applies most of all to life and to religion. What we need is not intelligence but blind faith. We do not need to understand but only to follow, and we can follow only one step at a time. We need simple trust that he who wrote the directions knew what he was doing.

Let us admit at once that it is often far from easy to do. We want to "choose and see our path." We want to be the architects of our lives and captains of our souls. We find simple trust and blind faith terribly hard to have when "the road is dark and we are far from home." Of course we do. The more complex the knitting pattern the more faith is needed. The more intricate a boat design the more trust we need. And the darker and more puzzling the circumstances of life the more we need faith and trust there too. We don't have to understand, but we do have to follow the directions, believing that he who wrote them knew what he was doing.

42

8
Following the Brook

In his novel *The Gauntlet* James Howell Street wrote about a bewildered young minister. When the story opens the hero is in college and is very much at sea both theologically and spiritually. He had been driven into the ministry by an inner compulsion which he could neither explain nor ignore. Now facing the ministry ahead of him he is seeking for some great river of truth, but has become disheartened in his search. About this Mr. Street made a very wise statement. "In seeking a great river," wrote Street, "he hadn't learned the importance of brooks; that the easiest way to find a river is to follow the nearest brook."

Rereading the novel I came across that sentence and then didn't read any further. This time that sentence was enough. It set me thinking, and I believe it is worth thinking about, "The easiest way to find a river is to follow the nearest brook." There is a lot of truth packed into that, even if it is not quite original. Ecclesiastes said much the same thing thousands of years ago. "All the rivers run into the sea," wrote the Preacher, which surely means much the same thing.

I began to think about being lost. If it did happen to me what would I do? James Street suggests an obvious and wise answer, find a brook and follow it, for all brooks run into rivers, and all rivers run into the sea. Brooks may wind and wind around, they may be clogged with logs, and their banks be heavy with underbrush, but brooks are going somewhere, they are off to join rivers. Rivers too are on their way to larger rivers, to lakes, and finally to the sea. In the midst of the wilderness here is something which is definitely on its way. If you follow the brook it will lead you somewhere.

Our pioneer ancestors knew that well. Rivers were for them the highways of travel and the means of transportation. But first of all they were the paths of exploration. Cartier followed the St. Lawrence to discover and found New France. La Salle followed the rivers to open up the great interior and discover the Mississippi. Champlain followed them to open up the north. Much later MacKenzie followed the river which now bears his name to reach the Arctic Ocean and later on another river to reach the shores of the Pacific. As Ecclesiastes says, "All the rivers run into the sea," so if it is the sea you are looking for a river will inevitably take you there. James Street is right. Ecclesiastes is right. Ask any explorer.

James Street, however, was not writing about exploring countries and continents but that much vaster and even more bewildering domain, the great eternal truths of God. He is writing about a man who is lost, not in the northern wilderness or the valley of the Amazon, but in the deeper and darker wilderness of his own inner search and questionings. The young minister of *The Gauntlet* isn't alone in such bewilderment. He has thousands of others who with him are equally lost, and thousands and thousands more who hardly dare to admit their bewilderment or have courage enough to start the search.

What really can we say to such people? I don't think it is enough to say to them, "Believe! Have faith." That is exactly what they can't do. The one thing they are afraid of (and I believe rightly so) is to put blind credulity in place of discovery and unquestioning acceptance in place of experience and conviction. No, it is not enough to say, "Have faith." Indeed it may be the worst thing we can say. Neither do I think it is sufficient to try to have them come suddenly from where they are to some other place. If waving a wand could bring them immediately from the wilderness to the sea without their knowing how or why they got there, their souls would still be dissatisfied. What lay between? By what way had they come? After all to reach the sea with any satisfaction we must know how we reached it and by what route, for the sea is not the only goal of our search, the way to it is equally important.

Well, then, what can one tell such bewildered people? James Street suggests that we point them to the brooks. Find a brook and follow it, he says, for the easiest way to find a river is to follow the nearest brook.

Yet a brook by itself may be a very small and insignificant thing. In an article in the *National Geographic* about the Mississippi, the greatest river on this continent, the picture which interested me most was of a canoe at the headwaters of that mighty river. The canoe barely floated on the tiny stream, its sides touching the bushes on either bank. In another article about the Thames there was a picture showing some people leaning over a spring, a tiny rivulet which could hardly be dignified by the name brook. Yet that rivulet, only inches across, was the headwaters of that river which flows past London and carries the shipping of the world on its broad bosom. A brook may be the merest trickle of water, but it *is* a brook and it *is* on its way to the river and finally to the ocean. So find a brook and follow it.

Flower in the crannied wall,
I pluck you out of the crannies,
I hold you here, root and all, in my hand,
Little flower—but *if* I could understand
What you are, root and all, and all in all,
I should know what God and man is.
—ALFRED TENNYSON

That's the kind of thing James Street was writing about, and also, when you think about it, what Jesus said in other words: "Consider the lilies of the field, how they grow." From that small anemone which he held in his hand Jesus pointed directly to God as Father. It was not simply a lesson he was giving others, it was the way he himself had come. He, who also had to learn, found the way to the Father through seed time and harvest, lambs lost in the wilds and a boy wandering far from home. Jesus also followed the brooks and was led to God.

There is not one who has not a brook somewhere near him no matter how lost he may feel. If he doesn't think so let him open his New Testament. I am not suggesting that he accept it all at once. If there are things which trouble him let him for the time being pass over them. Let him find a brook, even though it be but the tiniest trickle to him, and let him follow that. Remember that Jesus did not call people because they believed in abstruse or even simple doctrines of theology. He never demanded knowledge, acceptance, or understanding before they came. He simply asked of them two things, first to follow him and second to follow what he said. For example, when John the Baptist, imprisoned and bewildered, sent disciples to Jesus to ask whether he was the coming Messiah or not, Jesus simply said, "Go and shew John again those things which ye do hear and see. The blind receive their sight, and the lame walk, the lepers are cleansed, and the deaf hear, the dead are raised up, and the poor have the gospel preached to them." John was to follow a brook. That is a brook worth our following also.

Honestly now, isn't the trouble with most of our doubts and difficulties twofold. First, that we, being lost, are concentrating on the very things which hem us in—our doubts; and second, that looking for some great river of truth we ignore the brooks? What we need to do above all is to find a brook and to follow it. There it is at our feet, winding its way around the bend. Let us get up and follow it, for unless all the laws of nature and of God are overthrown it will surely and certainly lead to the great ocean of God's reality and love.

9

Jesus Christ, You Have Control

When I was a boy I read a story about a missionary. Not every story about missionaries interested me then or now, but this one did. He was John G. Paton, a Presbyterian, the first missionary in the New Hebrides, the cannibal islands of the South Pacific. I came across the story lately again in F. W. Boreham's *A Casket of Cameos*. I think you'll be interested in it.

It was in 1858 that Paton and his young bride landed on the cannibal island of Tanna to start mission work among those naked, painted savages. It seemed an impossible task and it certainly was a lonely one. It became much more lonely when Paton's young wife and their little baby died and Paton had to dig their grave with his own hands. But it was most lonely of all when tribal warfare broke out on the island and the savages in their frenzy threatened to destroy the mission and the missionary. A friendly chief, Nowar, came in the night and urged Paton to flee into the bushes and hide in a chestnut tree till the moon rose. Paton fled.

High in the tree he spent the night watching the savages beating the bushes in their eager search for him. "The hours I spent in that chestnut tree," he wrote afterwards, "still live before me. I heard the frequent discharge of muskets and the hideous yells of the savages. Yet never, in all my sorrows, did my Lord draw nearer to me. I was alone yet not alone. I would cheerfully spend many nights alone in such a tree to feel again my Saviour's spiritual presence as I felt it that night." Alone?

"Ah, but he was a missionary," you probably are saying, "a different breed from us." But read further and see if he was so different from us after all. "I confess," he wrote, "that often I felt my brain reeling, my sight coming and going, and my knees smiting together when thus brought face to face with violent death. Still, I was never left without hearing that promise coming up through the darkness and the anguish in all its consoling and supporting power, 'Lo I am with you alway.'" [1]

Paton was not different from us except possibly in one thing, he had great faith in a text.

But again you may say, "Well, he was a missionary, wasn't he? I'm not and you can't expect the same thing of me." Or maybe you dismiss it as pious religion, a thing to be expected of such people but which doesn't happen to ordinary folk and especially not to the virile and manly ones. Oh, doesn't it?

An air force chaplain told me of an experience which happened in Normandy after D Day. He was sitting in front of his tent when the alert sounded and the fighter wing prepared to scramble. The wing commander was racing to his plane but stopped for a brief moment at the padre's tent. "Padre," he said, "they say there are no atheists in the foxholes. I want to tell you there are no atheists in the cockpit of a Spitfire either." Then he ran on to his plane. Later that day they took Wing Commander Chadwick's body from his shattered plane which had been shot down. In his pocket they found the thumbed and well-worn New Testament he always carried.

"No atheists in the cockpit of a Spitfire," said the wing commander. "I felt my Saviour's presence," said the missionary.

[1] P. 137. Used by permission of The Epworth Press.

There is a third story which appeals to me even more, perhaps because it was more personal to me. When I first arrived at the Royal Canadian Airforce Training School at Uplands, near Ottawa, there was one flight lieutenant who took my eye. I was impressed by his look of competence, by the quiet confidence of his manner, and by the reputation he had for being an able flier. I was even more intrigued by a long scar which ran all down one cheek. How had he gotten it? I didn't have nerve enough to ask him, and he probably would not have told me if I had, but he brought the subject up one day and told me.

That flight lieutenant had been a bush pilot before the war, flying a sea plane with men and materials from a lake beside the railway to the mines and prospective mines far to the north in the wilderness. It was a risky business but it must have been interesting. Bush pilots, I have always thought, must be a particularly rough, hardy, and daring breed. This one certainly had been by all accounts.

One day he had a heavier than usual load on the plane. It was with difficulty he got it into the air. All seemed to be going well when just as he approached the railway bridge the plane was caught in a downdraft and he knew there was nothing he could do. Just before he crashed he said aloud the last words he probably might ever say or think in this world. He said, *"Jesus Christ, you have control."*

Then came the darkness, and after much darkness the slow and painful dawn in the hospital. Finally all that remained of that crash was the scar down one cheek and a memory—the memory of the words he had said in the hour of his emergency, *"Jesus Christ, you have control."*

"Lo, I am with you alway," quoted the missionary when the

cannibals shrieked beneath the tree in which he hid. "There are no atheists in the cockpit of a Spitfire," said the wing commander, racing to his rendezvous with death. "Jesus Christ, you have control," said the bush pilot as he slammed into the bridge.

I imagine that only a flier can fully appreciate those words. Training planes have two cockpits and two sets of controls. The student sits in front. Behind him, unseen, sits the instructor. Always that instructor has his hand near the control column, his feet near the rudder pedals. They remain near but not on the controls unless the student gets the plane into a stall or a spin or a sideslip from which he cannot get it out. Then at the last minute the instructor grabs the stick, plants his feet firmly on the pedals, and shouts over the intercom, *I have control!* The student on hearing these words is supposed to take his hand off the stick, his feet off the pedals, and to answer back, "You have control, sir."

That's what the bush pilot meant. Someone else had to take over, someone else had to get that plane out. He was finished, Jesus Christ had to carry on from there.

Missionaries, wing commander fighter pilots, bush pilots, yes; but what about you and me?

If there was a spiritual presence in that tree in far-off Tanna, cannot there be one in your home and mine? If there are no atheists in a Spitfire, need there be any in an automobile or a bus? If God can take hold of a plane (and nothing could ever convince that pilot that God hadn't), can't he take hold of a life?

But we must remember that if God is going to be able to do anything, he has to be *given* control, deliberately and completely. I wonder how many students and instructors have crashed because when the instructor called, *I have control,* the student was too terrified, too frenzied to make the response, *"You have control, sir."* Instead he froze to the stick with the grip of death and the instructor could do nothing.

It is not enough to say, "Jesus Christ, you have control." We have to give over control, to take our hands off and let Jesus Christ take hold.

10
Pie in the Sky

One Sunday a very seedy-looking individual came to the evening service and stayed through. That rather surprised me for, though I was more or less accustomed to people like that coming around just before service when they would be sure of finding the minister handy, none of the others had done more than ask for a handout and then run off quickly to the next church before that minister had gone into the service. This man, however, stayed all the way through, though most of the time he seemed to be either asleep or very close to it. He did wake up when the service was over and the expected happened. He asked for a handout.

I suppose I should have been grateful for his attendance, but two things got under my skin. The first was that he came to a service of worship not to take part in it but simply to use it as a lever for extorting financial aid which, judging from his appearance and his story, would be spent on liquid refreshment. The second was that in that service we were offering something of far greater value than what he was after. If he had really taken it, it would have made such cadging on his part unnecessary. I challenged him with both of these and for a moment I saw a spark of life come into his eyes and a response very near to the surface.

Then his face hardened again, his eyes narrowed craftily in their cupidity, and he said, "So you won't give me anything?"

I replied, "No, if you won't take what Christ has to offer, there is no use giving you anything else." So he, like the Rich Young Ruler, went away grieved, but he, unlike him, had no possessions.

Probably there are a good many people who would sing to me that bitterly accusing song of the depression about the church, which said something about "pie in the sky when you die," and scornfully declare that the church promises heaven after you are dead but refuses to give you anything here and now.

If that accusation is true, if Christianity is concerned only with the hereafter, with eternal life and many mansions, then it is a terrible condemnation. But to me it is an equally terrible condemnation if the church is concerned only with handouts, with the temporary alleviation of the world's difficulties. It seems to me that what Christ has to offer should be of real value both for this life and the next. Eternal life should make this life happier and fuller, filled with meaning and growth, and the discoveries and developments of this life should also be a foretaste of that life which is to come.

Thinking of my cadging friend, what have Christ and the church to offer him here and now? Peter in a similar circumstance told a beggar, "Silver and gold have I none; but such as I have give I thee: In the name of Jesus Christ of Nazareth rise up and walk." Now my friend wasn't lame but he most certainly was handicapped. Haven't we all been for that matter? Haven't we handicaps which prevent us from living happy, full, and successful lives? Lameness, blindness, deafness—these aren't the real problems which face us. I remember the commanding officer of an air force neuro-psychiatric hospital saying to me about the two hundred men under his care, "The problem with

54

every one of these men is spiritual." He wasn't what most of us would call a religious man, but he was right. The problems, the handicaps are spiritual. It was with my cadging friend and it is with us. That is the real sickness of the world.

Silver and gold cannot help here, indeed they too often only serve to make it worse. What Christ has to offer is the cure for the sickness. He seeks to get at the root of the problem and remove it. It is so much bigger than what we usually call sin, for his view of sin is deeper and wiser than ours. So often we only see the sins of the flesh. But with Christ sin is anything which prevents us from becoming the persons God knows we can be and has planned that we should be. Sin is selfishness, lack of faith, bitterness, resentment, hatred, meanness—anything and everything, no matter how small it may seem to us, which puts up a barrier against God and his purposes.

The power to break down these barriers is the first and most important thing which Christ and the church have to offer, without which everything else we may get is vain. What use is a million dollars, for instance, if I hate everyone? What use is the hope of life after death if this life is filled with resentment and spiritual misery? The cross and its gift of forgiveness is the clearing away of the barriers and the opening of the road to God here and now and forever.

The second thing is the promise of the road itself with all its discoveries. That is what Jesus gave Simon Peter, James and John, Mary Magdalene, and all the others who have followed him. As John wrote, "As many as received him, to them gave he power to become the sons of God." It is the promise of becoming, the lure to a growth which is infinite. Not only has what we were been forgiven and the barriers broken down, but he sets our feet on the road to becoming what only God knows we can be. Take a look at the drunkard in the gutter or my cadging friend sleeping in the back pew, three days' growth of whiskers on his chin, a threadbare coat on his back, and an opaque, lackluster, half-animal look in his eyes. That is what we see. But what does God see?

When we look at little babies smiling up at us from their cradles we wonder what the future holds and what they will become. We should have the same wonder as we look at the most disreputable looking individuals, for that is the way God looks at them. He sees for the worst of them a road to becoming, if only they will take it.

Christ also offers a goal and an ideal. One difficulty with so many people is that they have nothing they think worth striving for or reaching. Another problem with too many Christians is that their only goal seems to be that mythical "pie in the sky when you die." The goal Christ holds out is likeness to himself, to his courage, his manhood, his gentleness, his patience, his goodness, his heroism. Peter wrote, He left "us an example, that ye should follow his steps." Example without power results only in despair, but power without a goal is meaningless. Jesus gave us power to become and an example of that which he intends us to be.

Jesus also offers the company of those who are together seeking that goal which is both personal and universal. They encourage one another in the fellowship of faith in him. Bunyan's *Pilgrim's Progress* is apparently the story of one man called Christian on his way to the Heavenly City, but it is also the story of that man walking in a goodly company. I doubt if any man can go that challenging and testing way alone. We need others like ourselves to give us courage for the way which would be too difficult to climb by ourselves.

So here are some of the things I see which Christ and the church offer: the overcoming of the handicaps and the breaking down of the barriers, the power to become, an ideal and goal which are above all worth attaining, and a glorious company along that road to walk with us. These are the things I offered my cadging friend, goals for this life certainly and the greatest that life has to offer, but goals for the hereafter as well. They are bound together, life here and life to come, and both consist in Christ.

I hope that in a sense your hand has been out, for Christ has been offering something to you, the most valuable things in all the world. If you haven't received them already won't you take them? If you have, let us give thanks together in the words of Paul, "Thanks be unto God for his unspeakable gift."

11
Pink-Velvet Petunias

One spring day my wife came in with a box of petunia plants. On the box were two letters, "P.V." She said they meant "pink velvet." In my innocence I asked how she *knew* they were pink velvet, seeing there wasn't a sign of a flower on any of the plants. She sagely remarked, "Because that was the kind of seed the gardener planted."

Just so. That was the kind of seed the gardener planted. So he knew despite the fact that there were no flowers showing and despite the fact that all petunia plants look alike that they would be pink velvet, for he had planted pink-velvet petunia seed.

Immediately I thought of something Paul said, "Be not deceived; God is not mocked: for whatsoever a man soweth, that shall he also reap." In other words, it is an inviolable law of the universe that if you plant pink-velvet petunia seeds you will get pink-velvet petunia flowers, for that is the way God works.

It is strange, isn't it, that when we think of Paul's words we usually think of the dark side of it, that he who sows "to the flesh shall of the flesh reap corruption." Anyway I tend to think of that first and shudder at the words, "Be not deceived; God is not mocked." I find the law which Paul laid down an ominous one, that "whatsoever a man soweth, that shall he also reap." Now when I stop to look at it I realize that I have been very foolish. It isn't ominous at all. It wasn't intended to be. It is a simple statement of fact.

Really it is a rather glorious statement of fact. It says you can get pink-velvet petunias every time by planting pink-velvet petunia seeds. It says you can reap life everlasting by sowing to the spirit, definitely, beyond any shadow of a doubt, for "God is not mocked."

It is rather wonderful that in the realm of the spirit the same law applies as in the realm of gardens—that you get what you sow. If we sow courtesy, we get courtesy. If we sow understanding, we get understanding. If we sow love, we get love. It works every time just as truly as with pink-velvet petunias. Perhaps you say it doesn't always work, for you did sow love and all you reaped was resentment and bitterness and misunderstanding. Well, perhaps so, though I doubt it. So often I have found that people who talk like that actually didn't sow love and understanding at all. What they really sowed was selfishness done up in packages falsely marked. The package doesn't always tell the truth; it is what's inside which counts.

Even if it were true and we didn't seem to reap what we sowed, maybe we ought to go on to another admonition of Paul's, "He which soweth sparingly shall reap also sparingly; and he which soweth bountifully shall reap also bountifully." That also applies in the realm of the spirit as in gardens. It is not only the kind of things we sow which we reap, it is also the quantity; and if we are stingy in sowing we may not reap at all, for we have to allow for poor seed which may not germinate and for the vagaries of the weather. But if we sow profusely then we'll reap abundantly. Perhaps the trouble with people who complain about ill-treatment instead of courtesy is that they sowed one seed of courtesy to ten of rudeness. But if we sow courtesy bountifully, sow it broadcast, unheeding of the cost, then courtesy will grow up all around us in prodigal profusion. Love always surrounds those who sow love. They always reap the kind of thing they sowed in the abundance with which they sowed it.

In another place, too, Paul wrote of seeds and sowing. "But some man will say," he wrote, "How are the dead raised up? and with what body do they come? Thou fool! that which thou sowest is not quickened, except it die: And that which thou sowest, thou sowest not that body that shall be, but bare grain, it may chance of wheat, or of some other grain. But God giveth it a body as it hath pleased him, and to every seed his own body."

Paul was no gardener and certainly he was no farmer but he knew the truth of farming. He knew that sowing had to be wholehearted and sacrificial. You had to lose the seed, put it into the ground, let it die—so to speak—so that the spark of life in it might burst forth into new life. Yes, you have to throw the seed away.

One of the most exciting bits of reading I found as a boy was in Jules Verne's *The Mysterious Island*. One of the men marooned on that tropical, uninhabited island used to feed the pigeons back home in New York. One day on the island he found one grain of wheat deep down in the lining of his coat. One grain! He lost that grain too, for the leader commandeered it and put it into the ground. But from that grain came a plant, from the plant more grains. From those which they planted again there came a harvest. To get the harvest they had to risk it all, to let it die. They had to lose it to reap. You always have to lose what you sow if you are going to reap.

That is something as important to remember as the other two

verses. We reap what we sow; we reap it in the abundance with which we sowed, and we can only reap if we lose it and let it die. Jesus said that about his own life: "Except a corn of wheat fall into the ground and die, it abideth alone: but if it die, it bringeth forth much fruit." It was true for him. It is true for us also.

It is, however, the last part of that quotation from Paul which intrigues me most, that "God giveth it a body as it hath pleased him, and to every seed his own body." I wonder how pink-vilvet petunia seeds differ from seeds of other colors? It is not in weight or appearance or anything else which shows. Mix a gardener's petunia seeds and he will never be able to tell the pink from the blue or the blue from any other color, unless of course he plants them. Then he'll know, for in each is the mystery of its own identity. It will be what God intended it to be. In the germ of the seed is all that has been and all that will be.

How different is the plant from the seed. If you had only seen seeds could you possibly imagine what the plants would be like? Can you picture an oak tree from looking at an acorn?

Who, looking at these bodies of ours, can possibly imagine what "the body which shall be" will be like, the spiritual body as Paul calls it. But it is there, as truly inside us as the oak is inside the acorn, for if the seed is there the body will be there also. You see, it all depends on what kind of germ is in the seed. From that germ will come the body to be as truly and inevitably as that inviolable law about reaping that which is sown. "God is not mocked" here either.

We cannot understand either about seeds and flowers or human beings and the mystery of the beyond. We have to take it on faith and trust God who always works the same way. But we know that if we sow Jesus Christ, if we take him as Lord and Saviour, if we follow him, obey him, love him, and if his Spirit is in our hearts, then the seed of the spiritual body is within us.

That body we cannot see, what it will be like we cannot know, but if we sow it, sow to the spirit as Paul implied, then of the Spirit we shall reap life everlasting. "For whatsoever a man soweth, that shall he also reap," provided he sows bountifully and provided he is willing to let it die, trusting God who is never mocked.

12

He Wouldn't Go In!

I read about a man who refused to go to heaven because he had it on the best authority that there was music and dancing there! No, I am not being facetious. I'm quite serious. That man absolutely refused to go to heaven because he himself had heard music and dancing there. Of course there was another deterrent, too, his brother was there. So for those two reasons—the music and the dancing, and the presence of his brother—he stuck in his toes and refused to go to heaven.

I didn't imagine this. If you don't believe me turn to the fifteenth chapter of Luke, verses 25-28. "Now his elder son was in the field: and as he came and drew nigh to the house, he heard music and dancing. And he called one of the servants, and asked what these things meant. And he said to him, Thy brother is come; and thy father hath killed the fatted calf, because he hath received him safe and sound. And he was angry, and would not go in."

If this parable means anything at all, it means that Jesus was speaking about heaven, which is the Heavenly Father's house, and about that Father and his two entirely different sons. It is the best information we shall find anywhere as to why some people will not go to heaven. They will deliberately refuse to go, not that they will not be permitted to go. It is personal rebellion. They *won't go*.

It is strange how music and dancing are mixed up in this story which Jesus meant to be so much more than a story. One son would not go in because there *was* music and dancing, the other had run away because he thought that there *wasn't*.

But what of the Father, He wanted both sons. He was no heavy-handed parent, no stern discipliniarian. He had two boys and he loved them both. Reluctantly he let one go away when he insisted on going. When the other got angry and refused to enter he came out and entreated him. The father made no difference between the boys. He welcomed home the so-called bad boy, he begged the apparently good one to come in. He didn't lay down any conditions or make any stipulations. He implied that the door was open and that his own welcome was whole-hearted and sincere. Finally the decision to go or to stay, to run away or to return, was up to the boys. It always is.

But to get back to the music and dancing. The younger boy felt the father's house did not have enough of it. He couldn't cut up as he wanted to with the father's eye upon him, and probably also the elder brother didn't make life too pleasant in that house. Anyway he wanted to get away, to go where there were bright lights and joy and laughter and fun, and no elder brothers. He wanted to have a good time in life and he felt he had to get away from home to have it.

So he went where he thought there were lights and music and dancing and loud laughter and jokes and fun, as far away from the father's house as he could get.

A good many of us envy him. Of course not for worlds would we try it, but we do envy him all the same. We think that it would be grand fun if one had the courage to risk it. There is a strong undercurrent of envy of the sinner in the hearts of many Christians. Even a hymn suggests it when it sighs, "For Thee all the pleasures of sin I resign." The pleasures of sin! What excitement those words conjure up. They did for the prodigal. They do for many of us. We too would like to get away and enjoy ourselves.

Enjoy ourselves! What peculiar words those are, especially peculiar when we read in the parable that the prodigal "came to himself." "Came to himself!" He didn't enjoy himself *then*. He couldn't bear to look at himself. He didn't enjoy anything, for there wasn't anything to enjoy, not the pigs he looked after, the master who didn't even give him chaff to eat, the so-called friends who had battened on his bounty and then left him, nor in the memory of the pleasures of sin either. No, he certainly wasn't enjoying himself. The memories of the father's house were better. He'd go home. So home he went to find that all the music and dancing, all the lights and laughter, all the things he had run so far away to find were there in the father's house.

That is what Jesus came to tell us, that in the Father's presence there are "pleasures for evermore," that true happiness and real laughter can be found only there. The Father's house is filled with music and dancing.

That was the trouble with it so far as the elder brother was concerned, it *had* music and dancing. He could hear it. From the sacred portals of the solemn temple came the sound of lilting happy tunes. From the floor came the excited rhythmic tapping of feet. Every now and again came a burst of laughter, and underneath was a constant undercurrent of happy chattering as if the people there had not a care in the world. Happiest of all, dressed in the finest clothing and wearing a precious ring, was that wastrel, that scoundrel, that ungrateful, irreligious wretch, his younger brother. The elder brother boiled with righteous anger. He would not go in. He stamped off angrily into the dark and lonely night.

Jesus wasn't just telling a story. He was describing a world, the people in it, the God over it, and the heaven which was the Father's house. There were the sinful people looking for fun, the self-righteous people despising fun, and there in the middle was God. So the self-righteous elder brothers of the world, who were apparently so very religious, hated the younger brother, turned against the father, and stamped away from heaven. They would not go in.

It seems impossible. It just can't be. But it can be. Why was Jesus killed? In part because he was, in the Pharisees' phrase, "a man gluttonous, and a winebibber, a friend of publicans and sinners." He did unlawful things on the holy sabbath, like healing a man with a withered arm and making a blind man see. He forgave sins. He brought them an entirely different and undesirable picture of God, for he made God a God of love and forgiveness, a God who cared for Gentiles as well as for the chosen race, a God the gates of whose house opened to east and west and north and south and were never shut, a God who in Jesus welcomed home the prodigal with music and dancing.

In some respects this is a terrible parable—a tragic, tragic story. It makes me shudder. I think it made Jesus shudder too. John sums up its horror in a few words in the first chapter of His Gospel, "He came unto his own and his own received him not." That is the tragedy. He offered them heaven and they would not go in.

The horror and the tragedy still persist. They are with us today. The elder brother did not die two thousand years ago.

Maybe he will never die. He is still stalking off in rage, still denouncing the music and the dancing, still unrelenting in his hatred of the sinful younger brother. He is still refusing to go in, no matter how much God invites him, no matter how he comes out to entreat him.

What's wrong with him? Why won't he go in to heaven? It is because of that greatest of all sins—pride. In pride he wants to work out his own salvation, not in fear and trembling, but in vanity and self-righteousness. His pride wants heaven all to himself. He wants to stand up before God and say, "Brother." But pride can never enter there.

Heaven with its lights and music, its love and forgiveness, its happiness and joy, is for one kind of people only; it is for sinners. Only the prodigals may enter there or rather will choose to enter there, for only they can understand and appreciate it. For all of us who have been far from home, who have known what it is to be lost and desolate, who have finally come to ourselves, for all such there are the lights and joy, the music and dancing of the Father's house, and there is the Father who waits to welcome us home.

13

Doubting Your Doubts

Are you troubled with doubts? Most of us doubt some of the time. Far more people than you imagine have doubts troubling them a good deal of the time. In the secret hearts of some people, who seem to you to be so serene and untroubled, there are clouds of doubt at times so dark that they are almost overwhelming. So if your doubts have burdened you because they seem to cut you off from the rest of mankind and especially from the rest of Christians, take heart. You are not alone, not by any means.

Some time ago when I read Honoré Morrow's book about Adoniram Judson, *The Splendor of God,* I was amazed and concerned that much of the time while Judson was in Burma he was in a deep fog of doubt even about the very existence of God.

Adoniram Judson and his wife Ann arrived in Burma in 1813, the first Christian missionaries to go to that country. His career in Burma was hard. Persecution, imprisonment, loneliness, bereavement were his lot. Perhaps even harder was the long, long period when there were no converts and when the task seemed impossible. Hardest of all was his own inner nature, keen, seeking, sensitive, and doubting. In Burma he doubted. In prison he doubted. In his bereavement after Ann died, he doubted. Doubts were like a black cloud shrouding his soul and pressing down on his spirit. But all the time he worked at that which was finally to bring so much of Burma to Christ—the translation of the Bible.

When I read about him my heart ached for him. Poor Judson, filled with such high hopes and such great desires, plagued by doubt, and living in darkness of spirit, yet plugging away at his task no matter how dark the clouds. Yes, poor Judson.

It was a new thought to me when I read it that such a man as he, a stalwart of the faith and a hero of the missionary enterprise, could be filled with doubt. It concerned me, but it cheered me too. If God permitted him to doubt maybe God would not be so vexed with me if occasionally I wondered and if at times I questioned, yes, even his very existence.

The experience of another person helped me even more. It came to me in a flash one day when a woman soon to be a widow broke down and sobbed bitterly. As I sat helplessly by I suddenly remembered another who broke down and who had no one standing by. I remembered the sweat which fell in great drops of blood from his forehead, and I remembered his terrible words, "If it be possible, let this cup pass from me," and the even more terrible words from the cross, "My God, My God, why hast thou forsaken me?" Suddenly it flashed into my mind, "If God permitted his own Son to break down, if God permitted him to doubt, he won't be too hard on you and me when we do."

But that depends of course on what kind of doubt it is which troubles us. There are doubts which are simply excuses for evading duty and for doing what we please. Doubt which is just an excuse for license is not doubt, it is evasion. Neither God nor man can excuse that. Inwardly we know that we can't excuse it ourselves. The doubt with which God sympathizes and which, if the experience of Jesus be true, God forgives is the doubt of failure to understand, the doubt of a sensitive and burdened spirit, the doubt of one who above all wants to know and be sure. If that is your doubt then take heart. You are in a noble company. As they came out of darkness into light so can you.

There are some people who just cannot comprehend what I am saying at all. To them all doubt is of the devil. *They* never doubt. If that is because they are of that singularly happy group whose faith is serene and natural then all the rest of us can do is to congratulate and envy them. It may be, though, that they have no doubts because they have never made a real search, that the existence of God never troubles them because it doesn't matter too much to them whether he exists or not. Those we don't envy. We wouldn't trade places with them, not for all the serenity in the world. We don't want a mild acceptance, we want to know and to be sure. That pathway to certainty is no easy road I know from my own experience.

Well, what can we say to help ourselves? What can we say to others who live under a cloud and who, wanting to know so tremendously, are the more troubled because they don't seem to get any nearer?

One of the first things we have to learn is that faith begins with trust. That is important. Certainty comes from a hypothesis which is by no means certain, but which demands that we follow to prove it either true or false. Read the eleventh chapter of Hebrews again, that great chapter on faith. Do you imagine for a moment that Abraham and Moses and the others went out in a serene and unshakable faith? They certainly did not. They went out with a hypothesis, a suggestion, an inner voice urging them. They went out trusting that voice and seeking to prove it. They walked often in the darkness but they walked towards the light.

For us the important thing is not the question in our minds but the voice which urges us on. We must follow that voice just as Jesus and Judson and the heroes of old did. When Paul wrote, "We walk by faith, not by sight," he did not mean a faith that was an unassailable certainty but a faith that was an obedient trust. We follow a voice, we must keep on following even when the clouds are all around. We must trust, for there is nothing else to do.

The second thing I want to say is that so often the things which trouble us and make us doubt are things we are not yet ready to understand. We haven't grown enough for them. We have to walk step by step. If in first year algebra we opened a book on calculus we would be thrown into a panic, but if we go trustingly through other math courses in high school and university then calculus also will be revealed in due time as logical and possible. My most troubled times were when I didn't know how God was going to work things out. I could see today but not next year nor maybe even next week. I wanted to see clearly right through to the end, but God only leads a day at a time. He only opens the doors when we come to them. "One day's trouble is enough for one day," Phillips translates Matt. 6:34. That is true, but it is equally true, thank God, that his leading is also enough for the day. Despite your doubts you have enough faith for today, haven't you? Well then, walk today in the faith for today.

From Judson and Jesus and others I find this third important thing. Keep at the work which God has given you to do, no matter how you feel. Judson kept at his translation even when he felt he was almost an atheist. Jesus went forward to the cross, taking the cup of loneliness and braving the despair of spiritual separation from his father. So keep doing what is given you to do. That has brought others through; is there any reason to think it won't bring you through too?

Doubt and faith are very much like fear and courage. Heroes are not those who don't know what fear is; they are those whose knees shake and whose hearts fail but who keep on going. Heroism is the human soul mastering the fear which would destroy it. So also certainty is reached by those who refuse to let the clouds of doubt destroy them but who keep going on.

Faith after all is not our only concern. It is God's too. If we do our part he will do his. Our part is to trust, to believe that he will lead a step at a time, and to do now what is given us to do. We, like Paul, are to "press toward the mark for the prize of the high calling of God in Christ Jesus."

14
Don't Worry

About the best advice ever given to us mortals is this, *"Don't worry!"* The only difficulty with it is that so often we just can't follow it. Who really *wants* to worry? Who wants to spend a whole night tossing and turning, tormented by doubts and plagued by despair? Who wants to go around with furrowed brow and anguished thoughts? The trouble is that we can't help it. Certainly it is good advice for Jesus to say, "Take . . . no thought for the morrow," or "Let not your heart be troubled," and for Paul to say, "Be careful for nothing," that is, don't worry about anything at all. Certainly it is excellent advice. But how do we follow it?

Some of us, of course, worry about everything. Worry-warts they call us. There isn't anything we can't worry about—whether our tie is straight, whether we turned the oven off, whether we've got the train tickets. How often I've looked in my pocket for train tickets which I had looked for and found there not five minutes before! Calm and confident people look at us with amusement. But they'll worry too. Let them be in a hospital, rushed there by a doctor who explained nothing but simply said they had to go immediately, just as they were, that he would have X rays taken as soon as they got there. Then he went away leaving them with the calm advice, "Now, don't worry." Do they follow his advice? What do you think? The doctor knows they won't. He knows they won't drop off naturally to sleep, so he prescribes a nice little pill for them.

Those nice little pills, sleeping pills, tranquilizers, drugs—how many people depend on them, almost live on them! They are supposed to be an antidote for worry, and they do dull the senses and numb the brain for a few hours. But they don't stop worry for the subconscious mind is still working underneath.

There's an awful lot of worry in the world and the Bible tells us not to worry. It might be better, we think, if it told us how we could stop. It does tell us; it is almost the only place in the world that does. If we would only understand, follow, and believe it, our worries would be over.

Perhaps we approach what the Bible says with some reservations. It is all right, we think, for the Bible or Jesus or Paul to give that advice. Look who they were! If we were Jesus or Paul we wouldn't worry either. It seems to us almost like that doctor telling his patient not to worry. That doctor isn't on a hospital bed. He hasn't had X rays of which no one has told him the result. He isn't facing an operation all the more frightening because its extent is unknown. It is people like that who usually say so cheerfully, "Now, don't worry." What do *they* know about it? Maybe we think that Jesus and Paul were like that, so we are hesitant about taking their advice. What *did* they know about it?

When Jesus told the disciples to "take . . . no thought for the morrow" he himself had closed his carpenter shop, had gone out not knowing where his next meal was coming from, and had no possessions, no home, and no guarantee for the future. "Foxes have holes," he said, "and the birds of the air have nests; but the Son of man hath not where to lay his head." When he told his disciples, "Let not your heart be troubled," it was *he* who was going to die within the day, not they; it was *he* who was going out to be arrested, tried, and crucified. When Paul wrote the Philippians and advised them not to worry about any-thing, he was writing from a Roman prison while he waited to be brought to trial before Emperor Nero with the probability of execution at the end of it. Yes, those two knew about it knew far more than we.

With Jesus and with Paul it was like the patient telling the doctor not to worry. That is for me the one great reason I can take what they said. If anyone ought to have been worried it was Jesus and Paul and they weren't. They were calm and serene. They weren't pretending or putting on a bold face either. They really had discovered a secret which worked, which con-quered worry. It worked with them. They believed it would work with us. What was that secret?

In the sixth chapter of Matthew Jesus told his disciples not to be worried about tomorrow because of birds and flowers. To some of us it may seem childish. God feeds the birds, so don't worry. God clothes the flowers, so don't worry. Don't worry about what you're going to eat or drink or wear. Your Father God knows quite well how much you need those things. Just seek for his kingdom and his righteousness and he'll see you get all those things. That's the gist of it. That was the secret for him. He said it could be our secret too.

When he said, "Let not your heart be troubled," he added, "ye believe in God, believe also in me." Believe in God? Of course we believe in God, but does that stop our worrying? Jesus said it should. He said that in his Father's house were many mansions. Isn't one of our worries that we are going to get there too soon?

Paul's prescription to the fretting Philippians was don't worry about anything at all. Regarding every problem tell God all your needs in prayer and in pleading with special emphasis on gratitude and you'll find that the inward peace of God which is beyond all human comprehension will stand guard over your hearts and minds through Jesus Christ.

Somewhere there must be a catch to it. What is it? It is just this, running through it all, explaining the serenity of Jesus as he faced poverty and as he approached the cross, and accounting for the contentment of Paul in a Roman prison facing the possibility of martyrdom were two great convictions. It was, first, that God is God, the all wise, the all loving, the all powerful, who can and will control everything in the world for his own ends and purposes. Second, it was that they were the servants of that God, his very special servants, and his greatly loved children who were willing to be used by that God in any way he wished. They were willing to be anything, rich or poor, free or imprisoned, alive or dead, if it would help him with his plans. That is what is meant by "seeking the kingdom of God, and his righteousness"—being willing to be and do anything if it will help God. That's the catch. How many of us really and truly believe that God has the power, the wisdom, and the love they believed he had? How many of us, believing that, are willing to be anything at all if it will help God?

It reminds me of war. The enlisted soldier must be willing to be anything, to go anywhere, to have anything happen to him and to attempt anything for the sake of the country for which he is fighting. It reminds me of marriage too, for in true marriage each partner must be willing (no not just willing, enthusiastically anxious) to be or do or suffer anything for the sake of the other. And religion is those two things, a war against sin, suffering, and death—God's war; and it is love, the love of God for us, which made him ready to die on a cross, and our love for him.

David Livingstone expressed in modern terms what Jesus said so long ago when he said, "I am immortal until my work is done." Of course. It was God's work he was about. Therefore God marched with him through Africa and all God's resources were at Livingstone's disposal.

Do you want to stop worrying? Then here is the secret. Get on God's side without reserve. Then because you've done that, believe that God loves you, both because you are his child and even more because you are his servant. Believe that God knows what he is doing and will use you for his own great purposes. Believe that and your worries are over, for "the eternal God is thy refuge, and underneath are the everlasting arms." Then in truth "the peace of God, which passeth all understanding, shall keep your hearts and minds through Christ Jesus."

15

Deadly Suspicion

When I was young I asked a good many questions like "Why?" and "What?" "Who?" and "When?" and all the various combinations. People got tired of those interminable questions and often told me in exasperation that "curiosity killed a cat."

To me that seemed a very foolish remark that didn't make sense. So naturally I would ask *how* curiosity killed the cat. Whereupon I would be told, "Never mind, I'm busy. Run on and play." So I went off reluctantly, my curiosity unsatisfied.

Much later on I found that the statement is almost literally true. I didn't know then how curious cats are nor apparently did my parents, but I've learned since. Curiosity nearly killed one of our kittens. She tried to find out what were those two lights coming down the road. Fortunately it was the middle of the car which went over her, and the only harm done was that my shirt front was bloodied as I carried her in and that, after recovering from shock, she had to rest quietly for a couple of days on a pile of rags in the cupboard.

Curiosity *has* killed a cat, maybe hundreds of cats. I am certain it has killed a good many people too. There is something else, however, which is much more deadly and that is suspicion.

That is peculiar too, for while curiosity is the constant thought, "What is that? It may be interesting," suspicion is the instinctive drawing back and crying, "That is strange. It is probably very dangerous." While curiosity and suspicion are almost direct opposites and while it is curiosity which had been credited with fatal powers, at least so far as cats are concerned, I believe that suspicion is much the deadlier of the two and much more to be feared.

Suspicion doesn't usually kill people directly. It kills other things first, such as friendship, co-operation, and trust. It shoots its venomous darts into far too many marriages. If we were to count up all the wars which it has caused we could number its victims in the thousands and millions. Suspicion to my mind is one of the deadliest diseases on the face of the globe. Unfortunately at present there seems to be an epidemic of it abroad. One late example is that affair in Cuba. I don't know the ins and outs of it, but you could see suspicion sticking out all over. Castro suspected wicked old Uncle Sam and didn't trust him an inch. Uncle Sam had the worst suspicions of Castro. Both seemed to be right, didn't they? Of course they were. For what is suspected frequently happens as a direct result of the suspicion. People tend to act in the way we suspect they will. When we suspect something we make preparations to meet it. Those we suspect see our preparations and prepare to meet us. East and West are perfect examples of that today. The West believes Russia is ready to pounce if given the slightest opportunity, so the West prepares its stockpiles of atomic weapons. Russia sees those stockpiles, watches our armies, observes our long-range bombers, and doesn't for a moment believe our talk about peace. Perhaps we *do* mean peace, but then maybe so does Russia. You don't think so? You suspect the worst? Well, there you are. That's just what I was saying.

There is another reason, however, why suspicion leads to

79

strife, battle, and sudden death. Suspicion is an indication not primarily of the state of mind and intentions of the other person but of our own. Suspicion is a dead giveaway. Phillips translates the first verse of Matt. 7 in this way: "Don't criticize people, and you will not be criticized. For you will be judged by the way you criticize others, and the measure you give will be the measure you receive." For criticize or judged read suspect or suspected. It also applies. Then listen to a modern psychiatrist, "That which people criticize most severely in others is their own inherent weakness." What that means in modern psychology and ancient Biblical truth is simply this: We suspect people will act in a certain way because that is the way we would act in their place and the way we ourselves will act if given the opportunity.

Jesus and modern psychology agree (by the way, they'd better if psychology wants to be on the right track). What we suspect in others is what we unconsciously see in ourselves. That is what leads to a good deal of the trouble in the world. Suspicion reveals our secret desires and forces others to act accordingly for what they believe to be their own self-protection.

Is the only alternative then to be dupes and fools? Is there no middle ground between suspicion, armed and on guard, and simple trust which is constantly being taken in and made a fool of? Supposing there is no middle ground and no other choice, which would you prefer?

But there is another choice. For just as suspicion breeds suspicion, just as it reveals the secret purposes of one's own heart, just as it leads to the very things it suspects, so trust works in the opposite way. Yes, I know it is sometimes taken in and made a fool of, but are we not even more frequently rewarded by having those we trust come up to what we expected of them?

In Gal. 2:20 Paul explained how he became the man he did. He wrote, "The life which I now live in the flesh I live by the faith of the Son of God, who loved me, and gave himself for me." The other versions translate that "by faith *in* the Son of God," but I believe the King James Version is right, that it is the faith *of* the Son of God; not Paul's faith in Christ but Christ's faith in Paul.

Certainly we can see that in the attitude of Jesus to men. Jesus believed in men. It is almost beyond comprehension that God who knows men so well can believe in them, but he does.

There is an imaginary story about Jesus after he ascended to heaven. The great archangel met him and asked whom he had left to carry on his work on earth and bring in his kingdom. Jesus replied, "I have left the eleven apostles."

The archangel knew how human, weak, and untrustworthy they were and gasped. "But, your Majesty," he said, "suppose they let you down? Suppose they fail you? What other plans have you?"

To which our Lord replied, "I have no other plans."

Yes, God believed in men and believes in them still. When men have comprehended that and realized how great is that trust they have usually responded. It would be wonderful if we could copy Jesus on a worldwide scale, wouldn't it? That is beyond us as individuals at the moment, however, so let's stop worrying about Russia and Cuba and the Western powers. That isn't where the real problem lies. Let's go out into our own backyards. There's enough suspicion there to keep us busy cleaning up for a long time to come.

First we must come to realize what harm suspicion does,

how it has corroded our souls, and how it has forced others to act in the way we suspected they would out of sheer self-defense. Then, for realization isn't nearly enough, we must try trust. We must believe in people, believe in their potentialities, believe they will really be what they can be. Let us remember how God believes in us. Then let us believe that God's faith and ours can make what seems impossible come to pass. God has been doing that for endless ages now. He can still do it with us, with our children, and with those around us if we will only believe he can.

16
Exorcising Our Ghosts

It is interesting living next door to a cemetery. Many people who live on the streets to the west of us take a shortcut through there. Their proper way to the bus stop in front of our house is an extra half-mile walk. But they can climb a low wire fence, take that short walk among the tombstones, and come out a gate which is never locked and save most of the distance. So they use it and I don't blame them, though the authorities ever so often prop up the fence to discourage the practice. But here is the interesting thing, I have never seen anyone use that shortcut after dark. No, not even on the most brilliant moonlight night have I ever seen anyone scurry across that cemetery. If you asked them why they use it during the day and never by any chance at night you would probably get a lot of very logical answers. They might say they were afraid of tripping over the tombstones though, as a matter of fact, the path is quite easy to follow. Or else they might say they don't have to go out at night, which I don't for a moment believe. Or they might say they have too much respect for the dead, which they seem to forget during the day. I doubt if any of them would acknowledge that they had even the slightest suspicion of a fear of ghosts. Oh, no! But the fact is that they don't cross the cemetery after dark.

I wonder why and when in the dim prehistoric past we became so terrified of meeting a ghost? It even comes out in the resurrection story. When Jesus appeared in the Upper Room "they were terrified and affrighted, and supposed that they had seen a spirit." Three days before they had delighted in his presence. Now because he was dead, they drew back in terror. It was a ghost, and they were panic stricken.

If the resurrection of Jesus laid that ghost, so to speak, it ought to lay all other ghosts too. It certainly laid that ghost so far as Jesus was concerned. He came often enough, acted naturally enough, spoke clearly enough so that they were convinced that death had not changed him. What Hebrews says has a deeper meaning than most of us realize, "Jesus Christ the same yesterday, and today, and for ever." The same after death as before; the same now as then. His personality continued, the same personality only enriched and developed by the realm of the spirit. He wasn't different. He wasn't made terrifying and ghostly by his experience. He was the same.

That ghost at least is laid. In Jesus death and its changes have lost their terror. Jesus alive or Jesus dead and alive again is as loving and lovable, as friendly and approachable as ever he was in Galilee.

If that ghost is laid, let's lay other ghosts too. We all have them, haunting the back of our minds. They may be unacknowledged and unconfessed even to ourselves, but they are there. Unless all life is to be made miserable by that secret terror we have to bring those ghosts out into the open and look at them. It may be that when we do we will find, even as the disciples found in the resurrection story, that the thing we feared was not terrible after all.

If I speak feelingly about this it is because I was born timid I would hesitate to say cowardly, but that might be nearer the truth. Anyway I know what fear is, I was born with it. One of my cardinal fears is terror of heights. Not so long ago I stepped out on one of those balconies which sprout out from the new apartment buildings like kitchen shelves. It was on the sixth floor, and after one look down onto the street I drew back quickly into the living room. No, I don't like heights.

That is why at one summer resort my first task each day when I went swimming was to climb the twelve-foot tower and dive off. It was a very splashy dive, but neatness wasn't the object, just to jump off was. My knees might shake but my soul demanded that that dive be made. The first time I went about painting a house I climbed the ladder to the peak over the second-floor window three times. It wasn't till the third time that I managed to get a hand free enough to put on a lick of paint. I didn't like doing it, but I climbed and I painted all the same. So you see why I thoroughly and completely believe that we must lay our ghosts.

Perhaps the most haunting and terrifying ghost I have had was the fear of insecurity, of having no job, no support, and no prospects. That was one time when I said defiantly to God, "I can't do it!" It is not to my credit that I did, God made me. But when at last that ghost stood directly in my path I discovered that what Jesus said can be trusted to the uttermost, "Seek ye first the kingdom of God, and his righteousness; and all these things shall be added unto you." Yes, I learned that we can trust Jesus, trust him completely. That is a wonderful thing to learn, but it can only be learned by experience.

While not everyone of us fears to climb a tall ladder to paint a house, we all have ghosts. It may be that we don't think it is necessary to meet them at the moment, but even if we don't have to meet them, at least for our own self-respect and even more for the good of our souls we should face them. By that I mean we should acknowledge that the fear is there. Let's bring that fear out into the open and have a good look at it. Let's say, for instance, that we don't walk through the cemetery after dark because we are afraid, just plain afraid. Open confession is good for the soul. Ghosts, so the storybooks tell us, fade at the first blush of dawn. Well then, let's bring some daylight into the haunted recesses of our minds. You'd be surprised what it can do for you.

I have found that to do something about our fears is even more important than acknowledging them. I've met hundreds of people who chatter away cheerfully, indeed almost ceaselessly, among their friends but who become tongue tied and panic stricken when asked to stand on their feet and speak before those very same people! They declare that they simply can't, that they never will be able to, that it is utterly beyond them. No it isn't, it is just around the corner—a rather terrifying corner, I admit, but just around it all the same. By that same fearful path almost all public speakers have come and certainly all the good ones, and many of them, like myself, would confess even now their moments of panic when some important speech looms up.

When one of the most eloquent speakers and certainly the most brilliant person I know went north to his first summer-preaching field he said that, if there had been a train at the railway junction coming back he would have leaped on board. Terrified? I doubt if any of you have been as terrified as he was. Fortunately there was no train coming back so, despite his panic, he had to go on to that field, and so go on also to all the development of character he was to find and the contribution to the good of men he was to make.

Well, what are your ghosts? Cancer? Then shout the word aloud and face it. Death? Look at it now openly even though in terror. Helplessness? Look at that too. Then in your panic with the ghost gibbering at you, look at Jesus Christ. He came into the world to lay the ghosts. Put out your hand and take hold of his and then walk trembling through your cemetery. Instead of ghosts you may find it full of the angels of God and radiant with the presence of the Lord himself.

17

Stop Kicking the Cat

I heard about an office boy who kicked the office cat. It wasn't really the office boy's fault though. In some ways there was nothing else for him to do. You see, the president's wife had had a bad evening at bridge and the next morning she got up out of the wrong side of bed. Consequently she had several plain truths to tell the president at breakfast, and he left for the office with many things he'd still wanted to say left unsaid. On the way downtown traffic was hectic, with more foolish drivers cutting in and more traffic snarls than usual. So when he got to the office he was in the mood to rake the vice-president over the coals for lack of production, low sales, and several other things. The vice-president just said, "Yes, sir," and "No, sir," but when he got out he called in the office manager and gave him a blast for the good of his soul. The office manager then sent his secretary nearly into hysterics. The office boy happened to be passing so she vented her feelings on him. All that was left for the office boy was the cat. So he kicked it. It would have been a complete circle if only the cat had scratched the president's wife.

It reminds one of the stone thrown into the ocean, which is supposed to cause ripples which go on and on forever. Actually they don't, for friction wears them down eventually. That's where ripples differ from human beings. The upset caused by the president's wife is still going on. It didn't end with kicking the cat, it never does. It goes on and on forever.

But it shouldn't and it needn't. That is where Christianity comes in. Christianity is meant to put an end to those ripples of discontent, criticism, and bad temper. Don't let us be too hasty or too smug about it, however, for it is not an easy thing to do. In fact it is one of the hardest things in the world. But it can be done.

In common with the president's wife, the president, the secretary, and the office boy, we are all prone to relieve our feelings by taking them out on someone else. There was the man who had been sitting with his fellows around the stove in the country store and had been getting much the worse of the perpetual argument. About six he looked at his watch, got up, and announced, "I'm going home. If Martha hasn't got my supper ready I'm going to raise the roof. If she has I won't eat it."

You aren't like that? Well maybe you are not quite so open and honest about it. Perhaps you, like some of the rest of us, save up the resentment until you find an apparently legitimate excuse for blowing someone up. For in addition to our natural tendency for passing on our bad feelings, most of us also harbor a secret and humiliating knowledge of our meanness. So we try to save our self-respect and at the same time blow off our steam by discovering what looks like a good excuse.

Well what general harm does it do anyway? Isn't it just blowing off steam? Shouldn't people realize that and make allowances for us? The answer to both questions is no. It isn't just blowing off steam and other people have no more cause to make allowances for us than we for them. This tendency to take it out on other people is the cause of far more suffering and misery than any of us realize.

I think a good case could be made for saying that the real cause of the crucifixion of Jesus Christ was the passing on of resentment. Why was he put to death? For one thing he had offended the Pharisees about the sabbath day. Offended is a good word. You remember Jesus said, "Blessed is he, whosoever shall not be offended in me." Offended here means hurt feelings, bruised pride, cherished ideas proved wrong, and pet theories refuted. So the Pharisees were offended and determined to destroy him. The Sadducees were offended too. They were caught off base about that commercialism in the temple. They knew they were wrong but they weren't going to acknowledge it. What right had this carpenter, an ordinary layman, to criticize them? They'd show him! And they did. Hurt feelings crucified the Son of God, hurt feelings which people were too proud to acknowledge and which they had to pass on by hurting someone else.

If this business of kicking the cat is to be stopped it has to be stopped right within ourselves. There is no use our blaming the president's wife, the president, or any of the others. Of course we can all find ample excuse for hurt feelings; we can blame it all on someone else, but when it comes down to the center of things we know within our own hearts who is wrong. We are. The terrible cycle can only be stopped when we admit openly and honestly that despite all the excuses it is our own bad temper, our own meanness, our own desire to hurt others which is the real cause.

If we look carefully too it is our own meanness reflected in others. It is not enough to acknowledge our *own* sin; somehow we have to feel that we have had part in the whole thing, that there is something of us in the president's wife and in the office boy and, yes, particularly in the Pharisees and the Sadducees. The Negro spiritual presents a terrible challenge and accusation as it asks, "Were you there when they crucified my Lord? (were you there?)"

This is one way we can dimly understand the rather terrible and dark doctrine of original sin, that in a very real way we *were there*. We were there in the Garden of Eden. We were there at the cross. So in a sense we have to repent, not only for our own sins but also for the sins of the world, for those sins are our sins also.

Repentance and acknowledgment, however, are not enough. They never are. When you read the first letter of Peter you may find his advice to the early Christians rather hard to take. "This is thankworthy," he wrote, "if a man for conscience toward God endure grief, suffering wrongfully. For what glory is it, if, when ye be buffeted *for your faults,* ye shall take it patiently? but if, *when ye do well,* and suffer for it, ye take it patiently, this is acceptable with God. For even hereunto were ye called." There it is. Peter believed that Christianity could put a stop, indeed was called upon to put a stop, to this apparently endless cycle of taking it out on someone else. If Christianity can't do it, nothing can. Christianity can, but the end of that cycle has to come with us and within us. We have to pull our foot back and leave the cat unkicked.

I did say it wasn't easy. Christianity never is easy. It wasn't easy for Jesus either. When I consider all the wrongs which mankind has committed against God, when I stop for a moment to glance quickly over the world today and back through history and

91

then look up at God, I marvel at his patience. Think of the war, the murders, the cruelty, the blasphemies, and the filth. Think of all the evil there is and has been and then look at God. There you'll see a cross. You'll see men throw the Son of God to the ground and hammer nails into his hands and feet and lift him up and leave him to die. And you'll hear him cry, "Father, forgive them, for they know not what they do."

It did stop with Jesus. Stopped short. It must stop with us also.

Peter went on in his letter to write:

For even hereunto were ye called: because Christ also suffered for us, leaving us an example, that ye should follow his steps: who did no sin, neither was guile found in his mouth; who, when he was reviled, reviled not again; when he suffered, he threatened not; but committed himself to him that judgeth righteously: who his own self bare our sins in his own body on the tree, that we, being dead to sins, should live unto righteousness: by whose stripes ye were healed.

So it is our business to end this cycle of hurt feelings and passing on of meanness. It is our business because we are Christians, the followers of him who died for us. But we can't do it alone. Only by his grace can it be done. But he who did it himself can do it also through us—if only we will let him.

18
Contrary Winds and Handicaps

There is surely nothing in this modern age which can so bring us back into real sympathy with the disciples as going sailing. They too were familiar with boats. They had been brought up on them, earned their living by them, and surely loved them. For this business of sailing gets into your blood, so that you are never really as happy as when you are near the water or on it. I have never been able to discover whether the disciples actually sailed on the Sea of Galilee or just rowed. Yet they must have sailed a bit, even if it was only to stand high in the boat and open their robes to catch the wind and be driven along without effort. We do know Paul sailed or was sailed by others again and again across the Aegean Sea and along the east coast of the Mediterranean.

When we are out sailing we can feel akin to the apostles and strangely superior to them too. With the boat heeling to the pressure of the wind, the water foaming at the bow, and the waves sending sheets of spray over the decks we can be headed for a goal directly in the teeth of the wind and be quite confident we will eventually reach it. The wind being against us won't stop us. But it did stop the disciples.

After the feeding of the five thousand Jesus compelled the disciples to get into the boat so they might go to the opposite shore. Four hours later they were still in the middle of that comparatively small lake, toiling at the oars, and beaten by the waves.

"For," says the Gospel, "the wind was contrary unto them." That was the final disaster of a difficult day. That was the handicap they had never learned how to overcome. The wind was against them. That was what brought Paul to shipwreck too. He was on a large ship, holding 270 people, but even so the wind defeated it. It wasn't the strentgh of the wind first of all, it was its direction. They were sailing slowly along the coast of Crete when the wind changed and the ship could not bear up into it. The wind against it was the beginning of disaster.

Now we can't take credit for being superior to the disciples or to the master of Paul's ship. It is just that during the intervening years men have discovered how to defeat the contrary winds and how to make the wind a servant and no longer a master. Let the wind blow how it likes, the sailing ship can now go where it pleases.

Personally I like sailing into the wind. I like the feeling of being able to go where I want to, no matter what the wind does. To me that is the excitement of sailing. For speed or for getting to any particular place, a rowboat, a canoe, or the smallest outboard would be far more effective. But none of these gives quite the same feeling of mastery as sailing does. The wind is doing its best to blow me *down* the lake and despite all its efforts I am going *up* the lake right into its teeth.

How is it that we can do what the disciples couldn't? How has what was an insuperable handicap for them become an advantage for us? Today a ship is navigated upwind by a series of tacks, and even if she wants to go downwind it is done much more swiftly by tacking across wind. This maneuver has turned what was a handicap into an advantage. How? There are three reasons.

The first is that sails are now made to go against or across the wind, not just down it. They used to operate like umbrellas. Do you remember long ago sailing in a punt holding up an umbrella? It was quite exciting, but you always had to row back for umbrellas catch the wind only one way. So sails once did also.

The second reason is the rudder. Once all that men had were steering paddles or steering oars, great awkward things which really only worked well going with the wind. Now the rudder is able to hold the boat and to steer it and is large enough and strong enough to give the helmsman complete control.

The third reason is the keel. The keel digs down into the water. The wind blowing against the sail tries to force the boat ahead of it but it is met by a force which refuses to yield. The keel pushes against the water beneath the boat, and so the boat is driven not downwind but across it, even nearly up into it.

Sails, rudder, keel; these are the three things which have changed that handicap into an advantage, which have made the contrary winds of little consequence. That's what makes us feel superior to the disciples.

But *they* could give *us* pointers in other directions, for winds are not the only handicaps in life. There are others which are far more serious, which the disciples learned how to overcome.

Have you thought of their handicaps? The Jewish council looked at Peter and John and were rather scornful, for they perceived they were "unlearned and ignorant men." So they were. So were most of the early Christians. Paul describes them in Corinth as being foolish, weak, base, and despised. Many of them were slaves, most of them poor, and in the world's eyes of no account. Jesus started with fishermen, farmers, and tax gatherers. The disciples knew what handicaps were and so did Paul.

His affliction was possibly glaucoma, epilepsy, or maybe both. He describes himself in no flattering terms. There was little that was attractive about him.

Yet with these handicaps, with strong winds against them, those early Christians set out to conquer the world and in less than four hundred years, despite persecution and martyrdom, they had pretty well done it.

To me that is far more important than just sailing. How did they overcome their handicaps and turn them into advantages?

The three things which make modern boats able to overcome the handicap of the contrary winds apply here too in a figurative sense.

First their lives were altered, like sails have been altered, to accept the handicap and to sail against the wind. That is an important thing to remember about Christianity, that it is meant to fight against odds, to battle the winds, not to sail down them. Christianity doesn't change the winds to our liking. It changes *us* to face them. Unless there is a change in sails or in lives the wind still wins, for like sails of old the natural man just naturally drifts with the wind.

Christianity also gives direction. It provides a rudder which can control the boat and can hold it on its course. Christianity means a goal. The goal is up wind but it can be reached. If you are going nowhere in particular you naturally go with the wind, but if your direction and your goal is Jesus Christ, then you battle the wind to reach it.

And Christianity provides a keel, a foundation, something which refuses to be pushed around by any wind but which holds onto us and forces our boat ever and ever up into the wind.

For all who have handicaps (and who hasn't?) these are important things to remember. The handicaps need not overcome us. The winds need not defeat us. We don't have to drift or be blown wherever the winds want. We can win and were meant to win, no matter what our handicap, but it can only be done in Christ. He alone can alter lives so they can face the winds. He alone can give direction, and he alone can hold the ship of our lives steady on course.

19

Don't Let Go the Rope

A class of nine-year-old boys and girls in a town some forty miles or so from New York was to be taken by their teacher to visit a museum there. The parents were somewhat worried for it meant a train journey, a complicated trip across town, and almost a whole day spent in that bewildering city. They knew how difficult it was to try to shepherd even two small children through that maze, so how was the teacher going to manage forty? Teacher and class, however, seemed quite unconcerned about the difficulties of the adventure, so with fingers crossed the parents let the children go.

When the class returned the pupils were as unconcerned as when they left. One family tried to find out from their small son what had happened. He said nothing had. "But didn't you have any trouble getting around New York?"

"Nope!"

"But what did the teacher tell you?"

"Nothing."

"What directions did she give you so you could find your way?"

"None!"

"Didn't she say anything at all?" the parents broke out in exasperation.

The small boy looked at them in disgust. "All she said was, 'Don't any of you ever let go the rope.'"

If you've seen a small platoon of kindergarten children being escorted on a walk you will immediately understand. There is a long rope, any kind of rope. One teacher holds the front end, another teacher the back, and in between the whole class in two's, with the rope between them, hold onto it. That way they can be taken anywhere. They don't need to know where they are going, or have any directions given to them. The teacher knows and leads, the others just hold onto the rope and follow along. Everyone is quite safe. There is only one thing which matters, no one is on any account to let go of that rope.

I thought of that one day at a funeral service. Do you know of anything more bewildering than that road which leads to death and beyond? We are going off into the unknown and there are no directions which we can comprehend. The way is dark. It is the loneliest of all roads. Who can find his way through that maze? Who is not secretly terrified at the prospect? People come to ministers and ask questions, and we have no answers. We don't know for we too are mortal, we too go that same road, and we too have no directions. Sharing the same fears and the same difficulties, there is only one thing we can say, "Don't let go the rope."

At the funeral service I remembered that class of boys and girls being taken safely into, through, and back from New York without directions, without knowing where they were going. Then these words came leaping into my mind, "Yea, though I walk through the valley of the shadow of death, I will fear no evil; for thou art with me; thy rod and thy staff they comfort me." I thought also of the words of him who called himself the Good Shepherd, "Whither I go, thou canst not follow me now; but thou shalt follow me afterwards. . . . I go to prepare a place for you. And . . . . I will come again, and receive you unto myself; that

99

where I am, there ye may be also." Isn't that just another way of saying, "Don't let go the rope"?

Sheep are foolish creatures. They don't know where to find the green pastures. They are as likely as not to try to drink from rushing torrents. They get lost in the wilderness. They have no protection against the wild beasts. By themselves they are ignorant and helpless. But they have a shepherd; so they don't need to know anything except to crop the grass, to drink from the cool wells, and to follow sheeplike through the dark defiles. They don't need to know anything at all except to follow the shepherd, just as all that the children in New York needed to know was to keep holding to the rope.

But we aren't sheep or children, we are people. We ask questions as did the disciples in the Upper Room. We want to know, and we cry out with Thomas, "Lord, we know not wither thou goest; and how can we know the way?" Perhaps Jesus' answer, "I am the way," just confuses us.

Yet to innumerable questions and unsatisfied minds, that is all the answer we can get, for it is all we can understand: that Jesus is the way, he is the Shepherd, he is the rope.

The first letter of Peter has somewhat the same idea though expressed differently. Writing to the Christians who were so soon to suffer persecution and to face martyrdom, he pointed them to Jesus and wrote, "Christ also suffered for us, leaving us an example, that ye should follow his steps." Those footprints of Jesus are gigantic, too big for us to put our feet into, but as little children can follow after the footsteps of their father so we can follow the footsteps of Christ.

I think the explanation of what Jesus meant when he said, "I am the way," is that he is the path, he has blazed the trail.

That description would be more familiar to our ancestors in this country. A man's footsteps were soon obliterated, so how would you know someone had gone before or the way he went? But the pioneers left a sure guide. They cut blazes on the trees every hundred feet or so, permanent marks to guide those who followed after them. Walking through a forest is a bewildering experience. Trees hide the direction, the surrounding country, and everything else. All we can see are trees everywhere. But if there are blazes on the trees we know that someone went that way before and left a path. We can follow his marks and be confident of reaching safety.

Way, rope, shepherd, footsteps, blazes on trees—they all say the same thing to us, declaring that we don't need to know where the path leads, what dangers are hidden by the trees, or what the surrounding country is like. All we need to know is that someone went safely that way before us and that we can trust his leading.

This is particularly important to remember about death, that enigma we all face at the end. But why limit it to death? Are there no other bewildering ways through life? Certainly we should say to those facing death not to let go the rope, but what of those who are facing life? Thanks to God's mercy, death most often comes peacefully and quietly. It is life which so often terrifies, confuses, and bewilders. The twenty-third psalm has only one verse about death, the rest is about life. In John 10 Jesus called himself the Good Shepherd and said that he had come that man might have life and might have it more abundantly. The Shepherd who is sufficient in the dark defile of death is also sufficient in the mazes and valleys of life.

He is sufficient in the great open plains also. More sheep are lost as they graze on the open hillside than when they crowd together to pass through the dark valley and more people are too. In World War II they said, "There are no atheists in a foxhole," reminding us that in times of danger and darkness men cry out for a guide. But when there is no longer need for foxholes and the enemy has been defeated, men tend to forget their need of God. Those boys and girls being shepherded through New York probably held onto the rope tightly enough when the traffic roared all around them but I think the teacher had difficulty when they got to Central Park or when they walked through the wide corridors of the museum. It is not when the path is confused and all is dark that we need to remember the rope nearly so much as when all is apparently clear and safe and peaceful. The advice of the teacher is one we all need to follow all the time, *"Never let go the rope."*

20

Coming to Yourself

In a cartoon I saw some time ago a psychiatrist was saying to a very commonplace-looking man facing him, *"You* haven't got an inferiority complex. You're just inferior." What a slap in the face that was!

Many of us are troubled by what we are pleased to call an inferiority complex. Not that we generally have it right, for psychological terms are bandied about altogether too freely by us laymen who don't really know what we are talking about, but an inferiority complex is a good cover-up. It excuses shyness, haughtiness, unwillingness to take part in meetings, and a host of other things. I suppose we all have it to some degree, and unfortunately we seem to be proud of it. It is like the "drunk" who declares that he is an alcoholic, for while drunkenness is a disgrace alcoholism is considered a disease. How much nicer it is to call oneself an alcoholic and bask in self-pity or to say we have an inferiority complex and think that that excuses everything.

On the other hand the psychiatrist may have been looking at us when he said, "You haven't an inferiority complex. You're just inferior." Let's face that fact, it may be true. That would be a tragic discovery, knocking the bottom out of everything. Bang go our dreams, our ambitions, and our hopes. We get down to rock bottom and find that the fundamental fact is that after all we are inferior.

There are two terrible passages in the Bible about men who made that tragic discovery. One is in I Kings 19. Elijah had come from the apparent triumph at Carmel to find it was no triumph and that he had accomplished nothing at all, for Jezebel was still queen, still his enemy, and even more determined to destroy him. Elijah fled to the wilderness and there bowed down in the abyss of humiliation and cried out, "It is enough; now, O Lord, take away my life; for I am not better than my fathers." His lofty opinion of himself and his high hopes of doing great things were knocked on the head. He was not superior after all so he might better just die.

The second passage is from Luke 15 where the Prodigal came to himself. It took a pigpen and hunger and loneliness and poverty to do it, but there he was, stripped of all pretense and all illusions, facing himself at last, and not liking what he saw. He came to himself and cried, "I will arise and go to my father, and will say unto him, Father, I . . . am no more worthy to be called thy son." It was as if the Divine Psychiatrist had said to both of them, "You haven't got an inferiority complex, you're just inferior."

He could say that to a great many other people too, couldn't he? We see them every day, people who apparently don't know— but we do—that they are inferior. We feel awfully sorry for them of course, but that doesn't alter the fact of their inferiority. They may put on airs, talk in what they imagine is a learned fashion, preen and prance and pretend, and all the time there is that terrible truth they won't face that they are indeed inferior.

Perhaps you and I are inferior too. To a certain degree we all are. Isn't there always someone ahead of us, something we cannot do, some goal we can't reach? Thousands of people are eating their hearts out because of that kind of thing. Others envy them their success, yet all the time they are desperately unhappy because someone else has gone further and higher. The author sees another whose sales are greater. The artist squirms when another artist is praised. The popular preacher writhes when a rival's church is more crowded. We all know what it is like. It is a canker in the soul poisoning everything. The devil also knows. Tradition says that the once great archangel became the devil because he could not tolerate his inferiority to God. Jealousy and that is all it is turns angels into devils. What it did once it is still doing.

Speaking of the devil brings us to the one thing which alone can cure that curse of inferiority. That is the recognition that truly we are inferior to God. What a platitude! Inferior to God? We all echo, "Of course we are." But think about it for a moment. That is what Elijah had to do and the Prodigal Son and Simon Peter, who set out to walk on the water in the exuberance of his own pride. Each of these had to stop the parrotlike, unthinking echo, "Of course we are inferior to God," and realize that it was a fact. Elijah had started out to use God on Mount Carmel. The Prodigal began by using God. "Give me the portion of goods that falleth to me," he said, as if God's only value was to provide him with the opportunity of showing God what he himself could do. Simon Peter was jealous of Jesus who had come to the rescue of the disciples and tried to emulate his feat of walking on the sea. In each case and with us also it was failure to recognize inferiority to God. We have made ourselves equal to or independent of the Lord of hosts and from that very folly has stemmed our inferiority complex, indeed our essential inferiority.

If to recognize our inferiority is to cure it, it is not our inferiority to other people nor to any particular person, but our inferiority to God. To be inferior is to be less, but it also means to be under. God is our superior, we are his inferiors; he is our Master, we are his servants; he is our Father, we are his children; he is our Creator, we are his creation. A fact we too often fail to understand is that we were created for God and that God does not exist for us. It is not an easy thing to accept. Peter found that out. His last experience with Jesus was in Galilee where the risen Christ asked him three times if he loved him, and three times in response to Peter's declaration he said, "Feed my sheep." Then Peter saw John mournfully and jealously following in the distance and asked, "Lord, and what shall this man do?" and Jesus answered, "What is that to thee? follow thou me!"

Well, what is it to us what others do, what successes they achieve, or what positions they occupy? We have been given our own instructions, and we have our particular work to do. Jesus says to us too, "What is that to thee? follow thou me." That is all that counts.

It is my firm conviction that each of us, no matter what our particular talents or gifts, no matter what our position or our brainpower, has a particular work to do for God. It is a work for which we were created, for which we are being prepared and is made possible by God giving himself to us in Jesus Christ. No one else can do that work. If we accept that work we are equal to anyone in the world, because in doing it we have accepted our true inferiority to God, and when we accept our relationship to God we find our rightful place in the world.

It is only then, I believe, that we can comprehend properly what it means to be the children of God, for God's children are also his servants. They have been adopted not for themselves alone (what a heresy of pride that is!) but for the contribution they can make to God's great purposes. They are part of his family because they have part in his plan, and accepting their part in his plan they discover their place in his family.

Inferior to others? Yes, of course we are. There are many with greater gifts, many who outstrip us in what the world counts success. But if we do what God has given us to do we rank with any in the world, for God does not count success as men do. His only requirement is that we are found faithful in the particular task he has given us to do. Read the third chapter of First Corinthians. Three great preachers were ranged against each other—Paul, Apollos, and Peter. Paul squashed that odious comparison once for all when he said, "Who . . . is Paul, who is Apollos, but ministers by whom ye believed, even as the Lord gave to every man?" There wasn't any comparison because God appointed each of them. There isn't any comparison with us either if we too recognize and accept what God has given us to do.

21

What Are You Going to Do About It?

I suppose the hardest blows we ever receive are the blows to our pride. At least that is my experience. I well remember one experience. For the good of my soul I had been taking services in the county jail. I felt pretty good about it too. For several weeks we had been getting between twenty and twenty-three of the usual twenty-five prisoners out to a voluntary service. We were rather proud of ourselves, you know. There were five of us; myself who did the preaching, a friend who played the cornet, a Welshman whose tenor voice provided solos and kept us on pitch in the hymns, the secretary of the Y.M.C.A., and the grand old turnkey of the jail.

Then one Friday afternoon we came in to find without any warning at all that instead of the usual twenty or more prisoners there were just two lone individuals sitting on the bench in the shower room. The turnkey was dismayed. He hurried off to the cells to try to round up a larger congregation for us but he came back disappointed. No one else would come. The secretary of the "Y" looked at the two lone prisoners with disgust. Turning to me he said, "You can't preach to two. Stand in the doorway and talk loud so that they can all hear you."

I was sorely tempted, for my pride had suffered a blow, but my soul reacted against the suggestion. "No," I said, "I can't do that. If they don't want to hear I can't force it on them."

"Well," he replied, "what are you going to do then? You can't preach to two."

Inwardly I turned to God with a good deal of exasperation. He had let me down. He had failed me. He hadn't gotten the prisoners out. It was his fault. "Look here, God," I said to him, "what's all this? You know I can't preach to two."

Suddenly, as clearly as if he were in the same room, I seemed to hear him say with what seemed like a chuckle, "I *know* you can't. What are you going to do about it?"

"What are you going to do about it" stopped me right where I was. Maybe God hadn't thought we'd been so good after all. Maybe those two lone prisoners on the bench was his doing. Maybe he didn't really care if I preached or not. Maybe there were other things in his mind besides my sermons. Maybe he intended me to do something, even if it meant forgetting the other four and particularly myself. God had seemed to say; no, he did say, "What are *you* going to do about it?"

I looked at the prisoners and they looked back at me probably wishing that they were safely back behind bars with the others. Then I pulled my chair right up in front of them. I forgot my sermon, my prayers, my hymns. I forgot the other four, excluding them with my shoulders. I looked at the two and asked, "Are you Christian?" and one boy blurted out, "No! But I wish to God I knew how to be."

So I told them. For over an hour we three talked together. Forgetting all about anyone else, we talked about Jesus. The boy who blurted out his wish wrote me a letter from the Burwash Reformatory, his mother in Galt wrote me, and he wrote again a year later when he got home. I never saw him again but for that year at least he believed in and followed Jesus Christ. The whole tone of his letters as well as his words declared that. The other boy was a transient, in jail only overnight, and I never saw him again either. But if anyone was ever affected he was.

As I went out of the jail, the other four walking behind me, I spoke to God again. "Lord," I said humbly, "you know what you are doing. I never really realized that before. You knew I couldn't preach to two, but you knew I couldn't talk to two with twenty others there. After this Lord, you get the people. I'll try to do what you want done with them."

I think I discovered something that day we all need to remember, that God knows what he is doing, and I've proved it again many times since. His ways may not be our ways. They may seem dark as night to us. They may hurt our pride most fearfully. They may even seem to hinder God's own work, but still God knows what he is doing. I believe, indeed I know, that he leads us if we are willing to follow and anxious to serve him. He leads us where he wants us to go, leads us individually, leads us for each occasion. I think that was a tremendous thing to discover.

I found also that one can talk plainly to God, indeed one ought to. God does not want pious prayers and hackneyed phrases. That day he wanted me to say that I was bitterly disappointed in him, for I was. He wanted me to talk straight, for then he could talk straight back to *me*. I rank that discovery second only to the first. Do *you* want to hear God's answer? Do you want to pray effectively? Then talk straight to God. Don't hide anything, don't pretend anything. Just tell him what is on your mind plainly and colloquially just as you would to any other friend. If you do you may hear an answer, though it may not be the kind of answer you want. He is not likely to give in to you (what a foolish God he would be if he did!) but God will answer and that answer will be right.

The third thing I found out, after realizing that God knew what he was doing and had really done it—hurtful to my pride though it was—and after learning that I could talk plainly to him and expect a plain answer, was this: God expected me to do something about it. He had placed me in a situation and then, smiling at my discomforture, had said, "I know you can't preach to two. What are you going to do about it?" Now it was up to me. God had faced me with an unpleasant situation and expected me to meet it. He was implying that this was not a block, not the end of the road, but an opportunity. I've found it to be true a good many times since that the disappointment may be an opportunity, the apparent block may be an opportunity, and the sudden darkness may be an opportunity. That's the way God works.

It is a wonderful thing to feel that one is in line with the apostles. For instance there was Paul in Philippi, feeling pretty good after the conversion of the servant girl, feeling quite proud of himself because he had obeyed the Macedonian call, and thinking what great successes lay ahead of him. Then he landed in jail and was put in stocks in the dark and smelly dungeon. That was a terrible blow to his pride. That apparently showed that God was helpless or foolish or just didn't care. But you know the result; God had provided an opportunity. The Philippian jailer might never have had any other chance to find Christ. Then there was Philip after his great success in Samaria, also thinking he was pretty good and a really wonderful preacher, who was always destined to draw crowds. Then God sent him down to the desert where there was only one lone Negro driving home to

Ethiopia. Probably Philip had also thought that God was help-less or foolish, but again God knew what he was doing.

God always does know. He does with you. He's there behind you. He hasn't left you. He hasn't forsaken or deserted you. He's there, and even in your darkness and despair if you talk plainly to him you may see his smile as he answers, "I know, I know. What are you going to do about it?"

Well, what are you? Lie down and cry? Or realize that God is in this too, that he has led you where you are and for the sake of his glory and his kingdom has provided an opportunity right there. You may not see it, you may not like it, but it is there. Do something about it.